Market Entry in Japan

Market Entry in Japan

Theory and Management in a Turbulent Era

Ulrike Maria Haak

and

René Haak

First published 2008 by
PALGRAVE MACMILLAN

Palgrave Macmillan in the UK is an imprint of Macmillan Publishers Limited, registered in England, company number 785998, of Houndmills, Basingstoke, Hampshire RG21 6XS.

Palgrave Macmillan in the US is a division of St Martin's Press LLC, 175 Fifth Avenue, New York, NY 10010.

Palgrave Macmillan is the global academic imprint of the above companies and has companies and representatives throughout the world.

Palgrave® and Macmillan® are registered trademarks in the United States, the United Kingdom, Europe and other countries.

ISBN-13: 978-1-4039-9860-6 hardback
ISBN-10: 1-4039-9860-4 hardback

This book is printed on paper suitable for recycling and made from fully managed and sustained forest sources. Logging, pulping and manufacturing processes are expected to conform to the environmental regulations of the country of origin.

A catalogue record for this book is available from the British Library.

Library of Congress Cataloging-in-Publication Data
Haak, Ulrike Maria, 1965–
    Market entry in Japan : theory and management in a turbulent era / Ulrike Maria Haak and Rene Haak.
        p.   cm.
    Includes bibliographical references and index.
    ISBN 978–1–4039–9860–6
    1. Corporations, Foreign—Japan. 2. Marketing—Japan. 3. Export marketing—Japan. I. Haak, Rene. II. Title.
    HD2907.H22 2009
    658.8′40952—dc22   2008035151

10   9   8   7   6   5   4   3   2   1
17 16 15 14 13 12 11 10 09 08

Printed and bound in Great Britain by
CPI Antony Rowe, Chippenham and Eastbourne

Contents

List of Tables

List of Abbreviations and Acronyms

CNC	Computer Numerical Control
CPA	Certified Public Accountants
ESOP	Employee Share Ownership Program
EU	European Union
FANUC	Fujitsu Automatic Numerical Control
FDI	Foreign Direct Investment
FILP	Fiscal and Loan Program
FRI	Fujitsu Research Institute
FY	Fiscal Year
GATT	General Agreement on Tariffs and Trade
GDP	Gross Domestic Product
GNP	Gross National Product
HQ	Headquarters
HR	Human Resource
HRM	Human Resource Management
IMVP	International Motor Vehicle Program
IT	Information Technology
JETRO	Japan External Trade Organization
JMNC	Japanese Multinational Corporation
JPY	Japanese Yen
JUSE	Japanese Union of Scientists and Engineers
LDP	Liberal Democratic Party (Japan)
M&A	Mergers and Acquisitions
METI	Ministry of Economy, Trade and Industry (Japan)
MIC	Mobile Internet Centre
MIT	Massachusetts Institute of Technology
MITI	Ministry of International Trade and Industry (Japan)
MNC	Multinational Corporation
MNE	Multinational Enterprise
MOF	Ministry of Finance (Japan)
NC	Numerical Control
NGO	Non-Governmental Organization
NIE	Newly Industrializing Economy
NRI	Nomura Research Institute

OECD	Organization for Economic Cooperation and Development
OEM	Original Equipment Manufacturer
PDAC	Plan Do Check Act
POS	Point of Sales
PPP	Purchasing Power Parities
R&D	Research & Development
ROE	Return on Equity
SME	Small- and Medium-sized Enterprise
TPS	Toyota Production System
TQC	Total Quality Control
TQM	Total Quality Management
TRIM	Trade-Related Investment Measures
TRIPS	Trade-Related Aspects of Intellectual Property Rights
TSE	Tokyo Stock Exchange
UK	United Kingdom
UN	United Nations
UNCTAD	United Nations Conference on Trade and Development
US	United States
USA	United States of America
USD	US Dollar
WTO	World Trade Organization

About the Authors

Ulrike Maria Haak is an arts editor with the German television company ZDF/3sat and a journalist with special interests in the comparative study of different cultures, economics and the social sciences. She majored in Theatre, Film and Television Studies and German and Romance Studies at the Universities of Erlangen-Nuremberg, Lyon and Cologne. Since 1995, she has worked as an editor with the German television company ZDF for the culture channel 3sat, working on programmes such as "DENKmal" and "Bookmark – das Sachbuchmagazin" and is currently working in the editorial team for "Kulturzeit". From September 1999 to October 2005 Ulrike Maria Haak worked as a foreign correspondent in Tokyo (for the newspapers *Die Zeit* and *Der Tagesspiegel* amongst others). She has produced numerous publications on intercultural and international management, particularly in the context of European–Asian relations.

René Haak joined the German Federal Ministry of Education and Research, International Department, in 2005. Between 1999 and 2005 he was the Deputy Director and the Head of the Business and Economics Section of the German Institute for Japanese Studies in Tokyo, Japan. He was previously Senior Researcher at the Fraunhofer Institute for Production and Design Technology, and Research Fellow at the Institute of Machine Tools and Manufacturing Technology at the Technical University, Berlin. He has written numerous articles and books on innovation management and production technology and HR and marketing management in Japan and Germany.

1
Introduction

1.1 Globalization of the markets

Globalization of the markets, of production and also of many services offers opportunities, but also presents risks to companies with international operations. Business activities became considerably more internationalized at the beginning of the 20th century; the process accelerated after the end of the Second World War resulting in a period of radical breakdown and far-reaching change in the international environment in the final two decades of the century. Business activity at the beginning of the new millennium is deeply marked by these changes (Haak and Tachiki 2004; Haak, U. and Haak, R. 2006).

Against the background of this development, it is important for international companies to develop future-proof strategies which not only safeguard the status quo of their market position and their competitiveness, but also allow them to become more competitive and penetrate new and promising markets (Perlitz 1997; Hungenberg 2002).

Consequently, no international company can now seriously afford to neglect the dynamic Asian economic region. In this respect, Japan in particular assumes a key position because the Japanese market is large and future-oriented and its consumers are wealthy and sophisticated. The Japanese market offers international companies attractive opportunities and locational benefits which play a crucial part in setting up a business or in engaging in other forms of economic activity.

1.2　Japan – the largest economy in Asia

With a gross domestic product (GDP) of 4.976.797 Mio. USD in 2008, Japan is by far the largest economy in Asia. Its share of the world market is currently around 11 per cent. This makes Japan the second largest economy in the world after the United States. Despite the high growth in other Asian countries, Japan's GDP continues to far exceed the economic power of these neighbouring countries. For example, the GDP of the Kanto region (Tokyo and the adjacent prefectures) is larger than that of the whole of China. The second most important economic region in Japan, the Kinki region with Osaka at its centre, generates a higher GDP than India (JETRO 2005a, p. 5).

Several affluent groups shape the image of Japanese consumer society. These include the "silver market" with older and free-spending consumers and young working people who, often unmarried and living at home with their parents, have considerable disposable income. There are market opportunities mainly in high-quality consumer goods and in IT and communications. However, the automotive sector and its supplying industries also present considerable opportunities in Japan. The supplier industry in this case also includes mechanical engineering, which as the key industry for many other sectors has a decisive impact on the productivity and innovative ability of an economy. Japan has a mature and modern mechanical engineering industry which is developing constantly through innovative processes.

However, other industrial nations like Germany, Italy and Switzerland also have an innovative mechanical engineering industry which can use the opportunities offered by the Japanese market. Overall, there is great growth potential for companies engaged in mechanical engineering on an international scale as the Japanese manufacturing industry is very keen on improving productivity. It is important that international companies include the Japanese market in their strategies from the point of view of not only consumer goods markets but also investment goods markets (mechanical engineering, chemistry and pharmaceuticals, raw materials) when assessing an approach to international market cultivation and penetration.

There is another important aspect of business involvement in one of the most demanding competitive environments in the Asian economic region which must also be mentioned in this context. Business involvement in different Japanese markets not only creates growth potential for a company and therefore improves the profit situation long term; activity in a foreign and highly competitive market with sophisticated consumers and buyers also sharpens the company's own performance profile, which can then lead to exceptional performance. This improvement in performance opens up opportunities for market and technology leadership in less demanding and competitive markets.

Against the background of these various considerations, Japan deserves to be accorded special attention in the strategies of international companies which in recent years have neglected this economic heavyweight in their often blind enthusiasm for the Chinese market. The preparations for the Olympic Games and the media focus on China have boosted this development in recent years.

However, it should not be forgotten that Japan's share of global consumption amounts to around 20 per cent, with a population one-tenth that of China. Even if China and India continue to become more significant, Japan will remain in the world economy superleague. What is meant here by superleague? Japanese markets, Japanese technology and not least Japanese products and manufacturing technology set the standards in international business and its dominance of the emerging markets in the Asia–Pacific region is not insignificant.

Even though other countries in the Asia–Pacific region have followed suit and have started to close the gap very rapidly, it will be difficult for them to overtake Japan in the innovational core areas of industry. Development in many industry sectors and their key products takes evolutionary routes which cannot simply be copied and transferred. To draw level with Japan in product, process and innovation management requires more than just many years of high growth rates. It requires a tradition of innovation, which most aspiring industrial countries in Asia do not yet have. The power of an economy to innovate is rooted in its highly qualified people who are prepared to learn constantly both at and away from the workplace.

1.3 Specialists – a key role in market success

The recruitment of suitable specialist personnel plays an important part in the selection of a location in which to establish a foreign base.

Japan has a potential workforce of over 60 million. The high educational standards of the Japanese population are admired throughout the world. In 2003, the proportion of the population who had studied at university or a similar educational institution was 74.1 per cent (compare the United States with 60.4 per cent and Germany with 33.2 per cent).

At the time of the bubble economy and in the ensuing years, Japanese university graduates exhibited a clear preference to be employed by Japanese companies. As most blue- and white-collar workers remained with the same company throughout their lives, it was often difficult for foreign companies to attract suitable manpower. However, in the meantime, the situation has changed fundamentally. Pay and working conditions and not least foreign management role models like Carlos Ghosn have contributed to making non-Japanese companies more attractive as employers so that they are now also able to find highly qualified specialists and graduates to work for them.

These employees are not assembly workers, but the holders of expertise who develop their own brand concepts for the Japanese market. Localization of personnel and the consequent use of local knowledge for cultivating and penetrating the market are opportunities for international companies to combine the two aspects of "local trade" and "global thinking" which are often in opposition.

1.4 Innovative technologies

Japan's competitiveness is based largely on innovative technology and as such the Japanese government directly supports R & D. Total expenditure on R & D in Japan is around 3.2 per cent of GDP, which puts Japan ahead of every other industrial country, with many European countries lagging far behind. Even Germany together with France, Britain and Italy, the leading industrial and academic nations in Europe, cannot boast this proportion of GDP spent on R & D.

Japan also leads the world in the number of patent applications. Intellectual property enjoys long-term patent protection in Japan, which is crucial for both domestic and foreign suppliers of innovative technology. New laws are intended to ensure that in the future registration procedures for intellectual property rights are accelerated and disputes in this area are dealt with more quickly.

Japan has a dense road network, over 1000 ports, of which 133 are classified as being of particular importance for the national interest and foreign trade, and around 100 airports. The efficient rail network is famous throughout the world particularly for the high-speed *shinkansen* trains.

Because of its high gross national product, considerable spending power – Japanese GDP at USD 37 625 per capita exceeds that of the United States (2004) – and many globally first-class companies and research institutions, Japan will maintain its position as a leading economy even after the economies of other Asian nations have continued to grow.

With Japan currently in such good economic shape, we would do well to not forget that the process of modernization which formed the basis for its advancement to a world economy has only taken place over the last 160 years, after centuries of pursuing a policy of separation and isolation towards the rest of the world.

1.5   Economic boom and bust

The economic boom years up to the end of the 1980s ended with the bursting of the "bubble economy". The prices of property and shares, which had been inflated by speculation, fell to previously unheard-of depths. In the years of recession that followed, Japanese companies, especially the complex and interwoven *keiretsu* organizations, were forced to undergo restructuring. Many of the loans that had been secured so generously with objects of speculation in the bubble years now appeared as unrepaid bad debt in account books and made a major contribution to the banking crisis in Japan.

However, since the end of the 1990s the restructuring measures have borne fruit. The *keiretsu* have become leaner and have divested themselves of most of the unprofitable branches. Many banks are in the process of writing off the bad debts and are returning to profitability. Japanese companies with high levels of debt but which are essentially competitive are being given the opportunity to function profitably again through debt-equity swaps, for example, and through the measures of the Industrial Revitalization Corporation of Japan (IRCJ), a kind of trust company which takes over their liabilities and develops rescue packages.

These structural changes have improved the chances of foreign companies gaining entry to the Japanese market or improving their market position. Investors in particular are profiting from the Japanese government's objective of increasing the amount of Foreign Direct Investment (FDI) substantially over the next few years.

As a consequence of the crisis in Asia the Japanese economy shrank in 1998 and 1999. In 2000 and 2001, Japanese GDP exhibited poor growth rates of 0.4 and 0.1 per cent; it was not until 2003 that the economy started to make a significant and lasting recovery. In the last three years, GDP growth has fluctuated between 2.5 and 3.0 per cent. Economic growth slowed in 2007.

1.6   Return to economic growth

Stock market experts are amazed by the strong dynamics of the economic recovery. The Nikkei index has climbed to astonishing heights. The stock market reveals a robust picture. A clear indication of the revival are real estate prices in Tokyo, which are picking up again after years of decline. Newly built urban complexes such as Roppongi Hills or Shiodome are attracting interest with their offices, restaurants, shops and hotels. Japanese consumers, in many areas trendsetters for global changes, are gratefully welcoming the new towns.

Consumer buying patterns – Development takes a new direction

It is now certain that Japan has succeeded in pursuing economic growth again. However, only core sectors of key industries have been included in the upturn. Nevertheless, there are unmistakeable signs of consumer buying patterns gradually changing in the Japanese markets.

In recent years, the polarization of society and the growing social divide have also become topics under discussion in Japan. Compared to countries like the United States and China, however, Japanese consumer demand is still influenced by around 100 million people with a pronounced awareness of their middle-class status. Two key trends have become apparent recently. Firstly, the proportion of quality-oriented consumers (for example, of organic products) is growing and, secondly, the number of price-conscious consumers is increasing steadily.

In other countries, it is often observed that where there is less buying power, only cheaper products are bought. In Japan it is much more the case that customer loyalty towards cheap products rises as satisfaction with the quality of the product rises. Therefore, anyone who believes that the key to the buying patterns of Japanese consumers in 2008 lies in the division of society is risking the failure of their marketing strategy.

Where the consumer group concentrating on cheap products is concerned, it should be recognized that since the mid-1990s, Japanese industry has been progressively undermined, as China and other Asian countries manufacture products for the Japanese market which are cheap but at the same time high quality. Furthermore, the range of products on offer is constantly being extended. The case of the clothing industry is particularly revealing. Since the mid-1990s, more and more Japanese companies are getting their products made in China and in other Asian countries at low wage costs. At the same time, it has been possible to do away with margins for intermediaries by building up new direct routes for distribution. The success of the Uniqlo fast retailing chain is representative of this business model which has transformed the whole industry. It is not an exaggeration to say that casual leisure clothing that previously cost over JPY 5000 is now offered by Uniqlo and other companies for less than JPY 2000.

Under the influence of the ubiquitous Uniqlo shops, the middle and upper classes, for whom up till then "cheap equalled bad", were thought to be gradually coming round to believing "cheap but not all that bad". However, as Japanese consumers are exceptionally demanding, they are generally not happy with this "cheap but not all that bad" view. Many of the textiles specialists aimed at the success of Uniqlo and copied its low-price strategy. This resulted in even more competition amongst these suppliers and the increasing pressure on costs did not always have a positive influence on customer loyalty.

For this reason, recent years have seen simple low-price strategies abandoned and independent brands emerge. A market survey carried out in 2007 in which consumers were questioned in group interviews revealed that Uniqlo has been able to position itself not as a cheap brand but as a brand with the best customer loyalty. The respondents belonged to the group with an annual income of JPY 7 million, that is, a class with above-average incomes.

Companies in Japan which, like Uniqlo, have succeeded in building up a distinct market will probably be able to maintain their leading position in the Japanese market, but for companies under pressure on costs, it will probably be touch and go. Japanese consumers had just begun to have confidence in Chinese products other than clothing when they were deeply upset by a number of scandals in 2006 and 2007.

The Japanese felt that these events confirmed their view that "cheap means bad after all". This was highly damaging to the brands. It is unlikely that the Japanese will again be impressed by slogans such as "brand quality at low prices". Furthermore, products of acceptable quality or satisfactory function but without exceptional features only appeal indifferently on an emotional level.

The functionality of the product and the price are simply insufficient to motivate Japanese customers to buy. Essentially, Japanese middle-class consumers do not want a cheap product. They want a product with a good price–performance ratio and with additional value (emotion, image and so on) For this reason, the chances of European and American companies entering the Japanese market are particularly favourable, if they provide additional value for Japanese consumers. This is a value that they cannot acquire from native Japanese or cheap Chinese products.

For the European brands, the success in the Japanese market is based on a marketing strategy which can be described as the mass marketing of premium goods. According to marketing theory, it is easy to succeed in a mature market like the Japanese market in this way. Mass marketing means the strategy of not only addressing the upper classes that have been created as the result of polarization, but reaching as wide a circle of consumers as possible. For Japan, this means marketing to people with a household income of over JPY 2 million.

What exactly is a premium strategy? Japanese consumers see themselves as number one in the world when it comes to reverence for and readiness to buy luxury goods. This reverence and the motivation to buy luxury goods is based on the underlying desire to "better oneself" and achieve a higher status. For example, it is not unusual for students who do not have their own income to bring a Louis Vuitton bag home with them from a trip abroad. European brands in particular are the object of such reverence. Up to now it has been mainly expensive fashion brands from Italy and France which have prevailed in the global markets and which have done justice to the reverence for Europe with their luxury goods marketing.

1.7 Upturn – not an economic flash in the pan

Analysts at large financial institutions are assuming that the upturn is not just a flash in the pan brought about by programmes of governmental measures to stimulate the economy, but is based on fundamental data such as rising exports, more corporate investment spending and rising demand on the domestic consumer market. The demand-induced growth of the Japanese economy which has made such a contribution to Japan's economic success for many years has given way to a self-supporting process that owes its existence to the inherent dynamics of highly competitive and open markets. With much higher expectations of profit, not only are big industrial companies in Japan investing in high-quality new plants, machines and equipment; small and medium-sized businesses are also noting a distinct increase in orders.

Another indication of Japan's regained strength following the years of economic crisis in the 1990s and at the beginning of the 21st century are consistent surpluses in the balance of trade with the European Union and the United States. In sectors such as home entertainment, electronics and microchip technology, Japanese companies are dominating the market with far superior quality, in some cases to the point of a monopoly. In these markets, Japanese economic success is based not on the efforts of creative marketing departments but primarily on an ability to innovate that is way ahead of its competitors and which represents genuine added value for consumers. This means that the large product ranges, the high product quality and, last but not least, the favourable price-performance ratios offered by many internationally acclaimed Japanese companies are convincing arguments for many consumers to choose a Japanese product.

1.8 Toyota – a model for success and the knowledge of a special corporate philosophy

The success of Toyota in various markets throughout the world is a good example of this, as this showpiece business does not rest on its past laurels, but goes from competitive strength to strength in a continuous process of consistent self-examination and improvement. Consumers use their buying patterns to acknowledge these entrepreneurial efforts to improve the product because of which Japanese companies have today become the benchmark in many sectors. This means that companies operating at an international level must subject the strategies of Japanese success to very critical analysis if they wish to enjoy lasting economic success not only in the Japanese domestic markets but also in the dynamic and promising international markets.

For international companies, an examination of this corporate and innovation philosophy is playing an increasingly important role. Learning from Toyota means learning to win in international and sophisticated markets – and not just in Japan. Toyota's profits are rising year on year and it is expanding rapidly into a wide range of different markets throughout the world. New production sites are being constructed in the most important demand centres of the world. Innovative products and manufacturing processes underpin the expansion efforts of this Japanese automobile manufacturer which claims to have sold 9366 million vehicles in 2007.

This puts Toyota around 3000 vehicles behind its American competitor General Motors Corp. (GM) which has provisionally reported the sale of 9369 million vehicles for 2007, but on pure production figures for 2007, Toyota is out in front with 8535 million vehicles, 2000 ahead of the GM figures.

This is however not the only thing that indicates Toyota's rise to the number one position amongst global automobile manufacturers. Also, measured on economic data such as profit or market capitalization, Toyota is ahead of GM – and not just since last year. After Toyota built production sites mainly in the United States in the 1980s, and rigorously pursued a trend towards greater internationalization with new manufacturing locations throughout the world in the 1990s, both production and sales figures have improved constantly. Initially cautious involvement in China, which has increased since 2002, in West and Central Europe and in Russia and continued expansion in the United States have led to a more dynamic development than that of GM, Ford or Volkswagen.

General Motors, for example, relies more on cooperative ventures and company takeovers to expand and consolidate its market positions, whereas Toyota primarily relies on its own manufacturing and management expertise to continue its expansion. Early entry into the development of the environmentally friendly hybrid car also provided the company with fundamental advantages in international competition. The production and innovation policy embedded in a specific corporate philosophy at Toyota is playing a key role in its rapid rise to the top.

The management philosophy of continuous improvement governs all the decisions made by Toyota. For example, it puts together teams even at the production level. Organizing the workforce into teams is intended to improve the performance of the group members through communication and shared experiences (Suzuki 1994; Yamashiro 1997).

Toyota's management philosophy is based on the knowledge that it is not separate guidelines, methods or even tools that should be used to improve the performance of the company, but that all the components must be brought together in a complete context and must be used with deliberate purpose. This management philosophy, which is given its most striking expression in the continuous improvement process, stimulates and coordinates the motivation and creativity of employees, in order to improve employees' interest in creating value and to minimize waste. When individuals participate in the successes of the company they identify more with the management philosophy, which is not only limited to production, but covers all the sections of the company that create value.

However, value is also created by mergers and takeovers. Japanese conglomerates make a very active contribution in the international arena in this respect. Recently, Toshiba acquired Westinghouse, the American nuclear power plant constructor, for EUR 4 billion. Nippon Sheet bought the famous British glass manufacturer Pilkington for EUR 2.6 billion.

As business has improved for these companies, the labour market has also become considerably more relaxed. In 2005, 4.4 per cent of the Japanese were reported as unemployed, one of the lowest rates since the end of the 1990s. At the beginning of 2005, for the first time in 13 years, it was possible to offer a job to everyone looking for work. After a number of years with no increases at all, average wages rose again and large companies showed their gratitude to employees with substantial bonus payments.

1.9   Consumer confidence improves

It is not surprising that after long years of considerable restraint, these developments have had an affect on the consumer confidence of the people of Japan. It represents the largest factor in the growth of Japanese GDP. Whereas Japan's economic recovery originally depended essentially on exports and corporate capital investment, for about two years now consumption has also been contributing to the improving mood. Since the early 1990s, Japanese consumers had been uneasy. The bursting of the bubble economy, the Asian crisis at the end of the 20th century and the economic downturns in 2001 and 2002 resulted in more restrained buying. Fear of job losses, never before known, led consumers to deposit most of their income in savings accounts. This postponed consumption can now forge ahead.

Japanese consumer spending, which makes up a good half of Japanese GDP, leapt in 2004 by 7.2 per cent over the previous year. The last rise of this magnitude was at the end of 1982. Japanese consumers are spending more money on leisure, travel and home electronics in particular. Their buying is primarily quality conscious and selective, which represents a huge advantage especially for Western European and US companies. The government's economic policy is again creating conditions for robust growth. There are a host of opportunities as far as internationally operating companies are concerned; it has not always been possible to take this for granted.

After the Second World War, the Japanese economy hit rock bottom and many Western companies considered the Japanese market insignificant. It was not until economic growth started in the mid-1950s that their assessment changed.

1.10   The historical dimension

The most important factor for Japan's dynamic economic development after the Second World War was the rapid upswing in industry which was essentially driven by mass production and automation technology. The reforms undertaken during the American occupation were significant for economic growth in Japan after the Second World War. The deconcentration measures which manifested themselves in untangling the capital, organization and personnel-related complexities of the ten large business conglomerates (*zaibatsu*) created key conditions for the competition which underpinned the period of reconstruction and high growth until the beginning of the 1970s.

The boom in demand during the war in Korea contributed substantially to the recovery of the Japanese economy, which at the start of the 1950s was still unstable. After a short phase in which growth rates declined slightly after the Korea boom, mainly due to a fall in private investment, the period of the so-called "investment boom", *kôdo seichô* (rapid growth), began in 1956–57.

The high levels of investment were directed at the growth of heavy industries. The development of new products and the improvements in processing technology were at the forefront of corporate technology management. The aim was to improve production capacity and to drive forward the modernization and rationalization of production plants. Economic policy was set for growth. The strategic marketing of many Japanese companies in the consumer goods sectors directed corporate resources at market penetration and increasing market share.

Real economic growth in Japan between 1955 and 1960 was 8.6 per cent,[1] between 1960 and 1965 it was 10.6 per cent and from 1965 to 1970 it even reached an average peak value of 11.2 per cent. Although the period of high growth in the Japanese economy that lasted until the first oil crisis in 1973–74 was not free of cyclical fluctuation, the economic expansion of the 1960s was astonishing in view of the destruction that had occurred during the Second World War.

Until well into the 1950s, the predominant branches in the processing trades were those that had also been prominent before the war, such as the textile industry. However, in addition to the basic industries, the assembly industry, which included automobile manufacturing, electronics, mechanical engineering and precision mechanics, also developed into major vehicles for high growth.

The Japanese state supported existing and new branches of industry with tax allowances and by giving low-cost loans. Foreign currency was allocated specifically for the import of raw materials and up-to-date machine technology. Furthermore, large sections of the

---

[1] Annual growth rates of GDP in per cent.

domestic market were closed to imports and direct investment; on the one hand this was to protect the developing domestic industry and on the other the separation made technology imports easier because it restricted the opportunities for foreign companies to share in the Japanese market to technology licensing.

Seeing the rapid growth of the Japanese economy, many Western companies developed an interest in becoming a presence in the Japanese market, but the Japanese state had erected high, almost insurmountable obstacles to FDI. At this time, Western companies often had to be content with a minority holding in a joint venture with a Japanese company, in order to share in the advances made by the Japanese market.

At the end of the 1970s and the beginning of the 1980s, when the worldwide success of Japanese companies could no longer be ignored, US companies in particular felt that the way the Japanese companies were acting was a key challenge in national and international competition. Since the early 1980s Japanese companies had been attempting to build on their market power not only in Japan, but also in the United States. Extensive investment in production and sales facilities, a product and price policy directed at consumers and a corporate philosophy focused on continuous improvement *(kaizen)* governing manufacturing technology and processes led to a previously unknown improvement in productivity and quality through which the market power of Japanese manufacturers manifested itself in key sectors, such as the automotive sector, the electrical and electronics sector and many areas of the consumer goods industry.

1.11   The unstoppable advance of Japanese companies – learning from strength

The success of Japanese companies was not seen as an opportunity in those years. Western companies perceived established Japanese companies as a threat to their market position. More positively, Western managers saw in the up-and-coming Japanese companies a challenge that they had to meet if they wanted to maintain their traditionally leading position in key markets in their own country and in the emerging new markets. For more than 30 years now, research has been undertaken to find out why Japanese companies are so competitive and why they enjoy such strength and power in foreign markets but above all in their home market.

Numerous analyses and studies have been carried out that describe how Japanese companies develop products, open up new markets, organize work flows in industrial production and ensure the quality of their products. Investigating the causes underlying Japanese strength was considered a recipe that would allow a company to establish itself successfully in Japan, going "head-to-head" with Japanese companies in their traditional markets. Engaging in business in Japan is still considered extremely significant in the international business world and represents a special challenge for many managers.

1.12 The champions league of the international business world

Japan in many respects represents the premier league for globally active companies. Not only are the markets and Japanese companies' efforts in R & D significant here; Japan can also be seen as the most important "place of learning" for international management in the Asian economic region. It still holds true that economic success in Japan is seen as a special achievement in the international business world.

Western companies have been very successful and profitable in various ways in Japan for decades. They exploit the existing potential of the highly competitive, highly developed markets. Managing to adapt to Japanese conditions and the specialized market and competition requirements is obviously the reason for the success of Western companies. Simple business solutions and recipes are frequently inadequate. Long-established business practices and patterns of behaviour, even management systems and forms of organization that have been tested for many years in other countries, are not immediately suitable for use under Japanese conditions; they need to be adapted. Japan is often treated as an exception in corporate strategies for internationalization.

1.13 What this book offers

This book is intended to illustrate to academic and practising economists and social scientists the challenges, opportunities and routes to successfully doing business in Japan. It is targeted at

managers both in small and medium-sized companies and in large multinational companies, whose corporate and business strategies involve getting to grips with Japan. These companies might have exportable products or services or they are already manufacturing abroad. They have frequently gathered experience in other foreign markets and are now taking a tentative step towards a new and highly competitive economic environment – the step towards Japan.

Market Entry in Japan aspires to support both academics in their work on Japan and managers on their way to Japan and to provide them with help when they get there. The many and varied highways and byways of doing business which arise from entrepreneurial creativity will be made clearer with a well-researched and up-to-date representation of some of the more important aspects of society, business and management. Some of the idiosyncrasies of Japanese culture and society will be examined as will the development and organization of specifically Japanese management culture, primarily in the area of manufacturing companies. Last but not the least, this book offers a short but scientifically well-founded overview of the ways into the Japanese market that promise success.

This book offers support to those preparing to initiate business contacts and is a useful aid to continuing business involvement in Japan. The structure of strategies with which to negotiate and cultivate the market and recruit Japanese employees and the characteristic features of personnel and corporate management in Japan are just some of the topics handled in this book.

The aim is to improve intercultural understanding with well-researched information, practical examples and advice from the areas of society, economics and management and also to offer answers to the question of "How to enter the Japanese market and how to do business in Japan?"

2
Japan – An Island Kingdom with Many Different Facets

2.1 Natural and geographical features

According to Japanese legend, the Japanese islands were formed from the tears of a goddess which fell into the Pacific, resulting in a loosely spaced group of islands in the wide expanse of the ocean. The Japanese archipelago ranges from the tiny sub-tropical islands in the China Sea, of which the best known is Okinawa, up to the northerly cold island Hokkaido with its winter ice festival. Geologically, Japan was created from the huge movements of tectonic plates and volcanic activity which has continued uninterrupted to the present day.

Japan's coast stretches for several thousand kilometres. It consists of four large main islands:

1. Kyushu
2. Shikoku
3. Honshu and
4. Hokkaido.

There are also 6848 small and very small islands which are scattered over a total of four oceans:

1. From the East China Sea in the south, through the
2. Pacific Ocean to the east of Japan and the
3. Sea of Japan in the west to the
4. Sea of Okhotsk in the north off the east coast of Russia.

The whole Japanese territory covers an area of 377 899 km², which is slightly more than Germany (357 022 km²).

From the southwest to the northeast, Japan stretches along the east coast of Asia for more than 3300 km. In stark contrast to this length it is at most approximately 400 km wide, which is the distance from Berlin to Nuremberg. The capital city of Japan, Tokyo, is located at 35 degrees 41 minutes north and 139 degrees 46 minutes east, and is therefore more or less on the same latitude as Athens, Teheran and Los Angeles.

2.2   The forces of nature

Topographically, Japan is a markedly mountainous country. Heavily forested massifs dominate around 70 per cent of its total area. Approximately 7 per cent of the huge mountain ranges are considered inaccessible due to erosion and are left to the native Asian bear. Only around 18 per cent of the land area is under permanent cultivation, 11 per cent is meadow and pasture – mainly in Northern Japan – and only approximately 3 per cent of the land remains for central settlement areas for the Japanese population.

The consequence of this distribution is a huge concentration of urban settlements mainly in the flat areas near the coast, with Greater Tokyo with its 30 million people the most striking example of this. As Japan is so narrow and mountainous, the rivers are relatively short and have strong gradients. Their water levels are subject to seasonal fluctuation (snowmelt in spring, typhoons in autumn), which makes long stretches non-navigable for shipping.

There are 285 volcanoes in Japan of which 40 are still active today. Volcanic eruptions are frequent and still represent a danger to the population. For example, 43 people fell victim to the eruption of the volcano Unzen on the southern main island Kyushu in July 1990.

The best-known and the largest volcano in Japan is the 3776 m high Fuji-san, which erupted most recently in 1707. Climbing this beautifully symmetrical volcano, a national symbol invested with an aura of divinity, is still a "must" for most Japanese. It is possible to do this only in the summer months of July and August, when ascents are organized for hundreds of like-minded people and take on a carnival atmosphere; the rest of the year Fuji-san presents an imposing snow-covered peak.

Earthquakes occur much more frequently than volcanic eruptions and they represent a serious danger throughout the country. The most powerful earthquake of recent times claimed around 140 000 victims in Tokyo and its surroundings in 1923. Most of the victims were not killed directly by the earthquake, but by the fires that raged afterwards. As Tokyo was so densely populated and with the majority of its buildings constructed traditionally from wood, the conflagration spread almost uncontrollably throughout the city.

Many Japanese still check before they leave the house that the gas tap is really turned off, as leaking or damaged gas pipes or open flames can lead to serious fires even in small earthquakes.

In July 1993, 230 people died in an earthquake on the southwest coast of Hokkaido and 6400 people fell victim to the big Hanshin-Awaji earthquake in January 1995 in the port of Kobe. The serious earthquake that shook the West Japanese region of Niigata in October 2004 killing 40 people attracted some attention. In the comparatively densely populated Greater Tokyo, the number of victims was many times greater than this.

The Japanese government is trying to develop effective early warning systems, but there has been little success so far. Regular emergency exercises and constant improvement of rescue services are firmly part of Japanese everyday life and Japanese children learn very early on how to act in an emergency.

The Japanese authorities arrange earthquake practice exercises regularly in which Japanese-speaking foreigners can also participate. Anyone planning to spend even just a short time in Japan would nevertheless be well advised to get hold of information on how to act during an earthquake. The embassies in Tokyo often have leaflets on what to do in an emergency. For longer stays, it is advisable to buy a survival kit in a department store or to put one together: a small rucksack or bag with drinking water, a torch, a first-aid kit, a hard hat, preserved food and so on. Anyone working there for a longer period is recommended to find out from the local administrative offices where the assembly points are and to discuss with friends and family how to proceed in an emergency.

Foreign companies are also obliged to provide a survival kit with a hard hat for every employee at their workplace. In an emergency, it is important to stay calm, switch off gas, electricity and water, protect oneself under solid tables or doorways and once the earthquake has died down (they can often last several minutes) put the safety plan that has been agreed on into action. Rushing to escape outside can be very risky due to falling building parts or collapsing electricity pylons. In Japan, electricity and telephone lines are usually constructed above the ground attached to huge concrete posts. Landline and mobile phone networks cannot be used in an emergency.

2.3   The annual cycle of the seasons

The four seasons, which are particularly clearly defined in Japan, and the interplay between them have always played a major part in daily conversations, in literature and poetry and in the way people live their lives. The climate and the seasons should be fully perceived and felt emotionally and respectful reference should be made to them in conversation. Japanese poetry often refers to *shiki* – the four seasons – and in most *haiku*, the famous three-line Japanese poems, seasonal moods are often given concise linguistic expression. The Japanese people, who are mainly of an urban nature, pay great heed to the characteristics of each season: armed with photographic equipment or binoculars, the people feel it is incumbent on them to go out into the countryside or into parks and enjoy a fleeting encounter with the cherry blossom of spring, the narcissi and the lilies of summer, the glowing red leaf colours of autumn and the plum blossom of the Japanese winter.

Japanese cuisine is in step with the seasons. Further broken down into regional specialities, seasonal delicacies are served in accordance with a strictly defined ritual. At the beginning of the new season, it is important to change the scroll picture in the *tokonoma*, the display alcove, which is to be found in every traditional Japanese room – the *washitsu* with its rice-mat flooring. It would be a sign of extreme carelessness if a picture with cherry blossom were still hanging up in the alcove in summer.

In Japan, each season is assigned symbols from the plant world which are used for a variety of purposes and in a wide range of forms. It might be an icing sugar cherry flower with green tea or a red maple leaf as a design feature on a beer can, advertising that the brewery is also in tune with the seasons; whatever they are, these seasonal symbols are always charged with emotion.

The symbols used most frequently are cherry blossom for spring and narcissi and bamboo forsummer, while chrysanthemums and maple leaves represent the autumn. Plum blossom and pine branches are the symbolic expression of winter; on *o-shogatsu* – the New Year, which is particularly important in Japan – bamboo and skilfully woven rice straw are favoured.

January and February are the coldest months, and there is heavy snowfall on the side facing the Sea of Japan from Hokkaido to Honshu. This part of Japan is therefore often referred to as the Land of Snow (*yuki kuni*). The winter months on the side of the land mass facing the Pacific are dry and sunny, although no less cold.

Spring arrives in Japan at different times, depending on the region. When the cherry blossom first appears and where in Japan and which locations are most beautiful are favourite topics of conversation in March, April and May. Joy at the arrival of spring manifests itself in one of the most popular and most emotional festivals in Japan: *hanami* – cherry blossom viewing. Armed with beer, rice wine, Japanese delicacies and occasionally a mobile karaoke unit, people sit together in groups on blue plastic sheets, their shoes, of course, placed neatly next to them.

The dainty and fleeting cherry blossom represents, like Fuji-san, a symbol dear to the people's hearts of the beauty and uniqueness of Japan. Frequently, employees that have recently joined a company must secure the best places under the most beautiful cherry trees early in the morning; this provides their colleagues, who arrive after finishing their work, with the first indications of the new employee's commitment to the group and also to the company.

Spring is short, and battered by strong winds and rain, the cherry blossom soon falls. In June, the temperature rises quickly and the rainy season (*tsuyu*) begins. This starts at different times, depending on the region. At the end of June and beginning of July, the heat and humidity of the summer become stronger. Many foreign families living in Japan take their home leave at this time. The humid summer heat, which is accompanied by irritating swarms of mosquitoes, can last until September and frequently into October.

When the warm air masses move southwards in September, the typhoon season approaches. In late summer and early autumn, Japan is hit by an average of 20 typhoons. Some of them pass by the Japanese land mass, while others collide at full speed with the mainland and leave a trail of destruction. Flights are cancelled, ships stay in their harbours, and public transport, both national and local, are disrupted. When typhoons threaten, the Japanese *shinkansen* high-speed trains remain in the safety of their stations. The heavy typhoon rainfall can cause whole masses of earth to slide and devastate roads, power lines and residential areas.

Typhoon warnings issued by the authorities should always be heeded. It is unsafe to go outside until the official all-clear. A personal assessment can be deceptive, because in the calm "eye" of the typhoon, that is its centre, the rainfall stops and the wind drops briefly, only to break out again with full impact. Always remember, personal safety is more important than business appointments, particularly since only limited travel on public transport is possible when there is a danger of a typhoon. Even public events, such as concerts, receptions or conferences are often cancelled when a typhoon threatens. The media issue regular reports on the size, route and development of typhoons.

The Japanese media carry a lot of information about the annual autumn storms and all Japanese people take weather forecasts and warnings very seriously. Foreign visitors should postpone their visit when there are typhoon warnings, particularly since the Japanese will also change their schedules. Every Japanese business partner will understand if you cancel or postpone a business appointment because of a typhoon warning.

Despite the typhoons, the autumn is warm and sunny until well into December. In the same way as viewing the cherry blossom blooming in spring, admiring the autumn colour is part of the autumn. At the beginning of October, the Japanese maple, *momiji*, starts to glow yellow, orange and red and attracts countless Japanese tourists, especially on the island of Miyajima, in Nagano prefecture and in Kyoto. The Japanese word for autumnal colour is *koyo*, but *momiji* is used more frequently as a synonym for the autumn leaves. Trips in autumn to view the colourful foliage have been given their own name: *momiji gari*, which roughly translates as "chasing the autumn leaves".

It is a good idea to plan a first business trip in November; with its climate and beauty, the Japanese consider autumn their showcase season. There is no summer heat, no annoying swarms of mosquitoes and no natural dangers (except for the ever-present threat of earthquakes). It is not by chance that with its colourful foliage and atmospheric light the autumn is the best time for even the Japanese to take a romantic trip to the cultural city of Kyoto. It is possible to combine business and pleasure very enjoyably in the last four months of the year. A round of golf with the Japanese partner or a visit together to a temple, a shrine or a Japanese garden following initial discussions or after closing a deal will cement personal relationships and deepen mutual trust.

As the last month of the year, December, also known as *shiwasu*, increases the pressure to fully meet every obligation so that nothing negative is taken into the new year. The preparations for the New Year festivities, *o-shogatsu,* make great demands on many Japanese people. Japanese business partners are faced with a huge programme of compulsory duties in December: New Year greetings, *nengajo*, must be sent; end-of-year presents, *o-seibo,* procured for supervisors, colleagues and customers; in short, anyone to whom one has felt indebted over the year for whatever reason. In order to make it easier to express this form of esteem, many Japanese department stores offer pre-prepared gift packages in departments set up especially for this purpose; these are frequently foodstuffs available for JPY 3000–15 000.

In Japan New Year's Eve, *omisoka*, is spent quietly with the family or close friends. There are no fireworks. Before this, there are lively and lavish festivities at the workplace with colleagues held under the motto "forget the old year", *bonenkai*. The New Year begins with the traditional New Year's Eve dish of buckwheat noodles, *toshikoshi-soba*, which represents health and a long life.

2.4   A short history of Japan

Japan has a rich history that goes back several thousand years. Finds of early Japanese pottery illustrate the creativity of long-past times. However, it was only with the introduction of Buddhism in the 7th century that Japan's history was also recorded in writing.

The era of the Tokugawa shogunate, 1600–1850, was very significant. During these 250 years or so, Japan had little contact with the rest of the world. In order not to be completely cut off from global developments, an artificial island was created in the harbour of Nagasaki, Dejima, which was intended for foreigners. Only the Dutch were allowed to trade with Japan and they passed on technical expertise and knowledge in the areas of medicine, chemistry and astronomy.

Under the Tokugawa family shogunate, the population was grouped into a hierarchy of four classes:

1. the Samurai
2. the farmers
3. the artisans, and
4. on the lowest level, the traders.

They nevertheless were able to exercise a certain amount of influence with their financial resources. Only the nobility were higher on the social pyramid than the class of the Samurai.

Opening up to the West

The year 1853 marked a turning point in the history of Japan: American warships sailed into the Bay of Tokyo and under the command of Commodore Perry forced Japan to open up its ports and to start trading with the West. The period of isolation of Japan under the rule of individual families was at an end. Some years of political unrest followed, in which a few Samurai and *daimyo* (territorial lords) campaigned for a new shogunate and others supported the re-establishment of the Emperor who for centuries had played only a subordinate political role (Schwalbe 1989).

The so-called 'Meiji restoration' saw a fundamental handover of power and therefore the start of a new era in 1868, which meant the end of the shogunate. At the age of 17, Emperor Meiji became the Head of State and the imperial capital was moved from Kyoto to Edo, which from then on was named Tokyo (eastern capital). The modernization of Japan began in the Meiji era during the second half of the 19th century.

In a true frenzy of Westernization, experts from a wide range of disciplines such as law, political science, school systems and education, architecture and art, medicine and health were brought from Europe and the United States to Japan to act as advisors and role models. Even then the aim of these efforts was total perfection and to use the best results from the fields of international research and to adapt the most promising developments in every discipline to the sensibilities and the special characteristics of Japan.

During the Taisho era (1912–26) Japan was involved in the First World War. Outwardly this brought Japan recognition as the fifth major power and the military secured its dominant position at home. In the 1920s and 1930s, Japan pursued an aggressive nationalist foreign policy which culminated in an alliance with Nazi Germany during the Second World War.

Japan's military regime capitulated after the Americans dropped atomic bombs on Hiroshima and Nagasaki on 15 August 1945. Seven years of American occupation followed, which ended in 1952 with the Peace Treaty of San Francisco. In 1947 the first post-war parliament was elected by the people and since then Japan's politics have been determined by prime ministers, who, with a ten-month exception, have always appointed cabinets controlled by the parliamentary majority of the Liberal Democratic Party (LDP). The United States continues to wield substantial influence in economic and political circles.

The Relationship with China

Japanese–Chinese relations are a special case. They are characterized by strong economic interests on both sides, political scepticism and historically justified suspicion on the part of China given the atrocities committed by Japanese forces during the Second World War. Every Japanese government so far has refused to offer the official apology demanded by China.

After the Second World War, tensions between China and Japan increased. China therefore seemed inaccessible as a market and as a supplier of resources for Japanese companies for years, even decades. A period of re-orientation followed, in which the United States became a reliable partner in the course of Japan's economic recovery.

Since the 1950s, Japan has achieved high growth rates, with some Japanese companies rapidly becoming world leaders. As a consequence, China saw Japan as a potential source of up-to-date production technology and modern investment goods for its own technological and economic development which would be accessible only if relations were normalized (Haak and Hilpert 2003).

Furthermore, Japan would only be able to provide development aid if there were an improvement in the political relationship between the two countries. Today, the strategies of international Japanese companies would be unthinkable without China as a production base and a market (Haak and Tachiki 2004).

3
Society in the 21st Century

3.1 The imperial dynasty

Japan presents itself today as a centrally governed state. The current constitution (*nihon koku kempo*), which became the basis for the creation of a democratic society, was written with the assistance of the victorious Americans and replaced the 1889 Meiji constitution, coming into force in May 1947. After the war, the Emperor foreswore his godlike status, but he is still considered the highest symbol of the state (Schwalbe 1989).

One peculiarity of Japan is its calendar, which is based on the years reigned by each emperor and runs parallel to the Western calendar. Each reign is given a motto-like statement. For example, the nationalistic attempts to expand in the 1930s and 1940s and during the Second World War fell, significantly, in the Hirohito era (1926–89), which was called *showa*, "Enlightened Peace". The current Emperor Akihito succeeded his father Hirohito in 1989 and founded the *heisei* calendar (which roughly translates as "to create peace").

In this parliamentary democratic monarchy, the Emperor primarily carries out official representation duties, but can cautiously edge the monarchy towards a more liberal structure within the very limited opportunities allowed by the ultraconservative court. For example, in the face of disapproval openly expressed by the court, Emperor Akihito married an untitled woman; his son, Crown Prince Naruhito followed suit (Haak, U. 2001d).

Unlike the Europeans and Americans, the Japanese are sensitive regarding humour involving their government or the imperial family. Remarks conveying negative, joking or ironic sentiments about Japanese politics, administration or the imperial family are best not made, even in relaxed social surroundings. Several years ago, diplomatic protests and apologies resulted when the former *Süddeutsche Zeitung* magazine carried a front-page story about the Crown Prince and his wife that included satirical and ironic allusions to their long-standing problems in producing an heir.

3.2   The constitution

Important aspects of the constitution are

- the separation of power,
- the renunciation of offensive warfare and
- the guarantee of human rights.

The Diet (*kokkai*) is the highest organ of the state. It is elected in a general and secret ballot and consists of two chambers.

The Lower House (members elected for four years) is responsible for legislation whereas the Upper House (members elected for six years) has an advisory function.

The prime minister, who is selected by the Diet, appoints the ministers to his cabinet, which exercises governmental power. It is answerable to the Diet and not to the Emperor and can be forced to resign by a vote of no confidence. Men and women have the right to vote after they have completed their twentieth year.

Generally there is no compulsory military service. The deployment of the so-called "defence troops" abroad has been under discussion for years and has again become highly charged against the background of the American activities in Iraq. For the first time since the Second World War, Japanese soldiers were deployed there after the war, their remit being to support their US allies in humanitarian tasks rather than actual self-defence. After the *tsunami* in the Indian Ocean, which swept more than 230 000 people to death in December 2004, Japan sent almost a thousand soldiers, the largest contingent since the Second World War, to Indonesia in order to give humanitarian aid.

The pacifist principle laid down in Article 9 of the constitution, which allows the Japanese government to at most defend its country, but excludes categorically any other form of military deployment, is currently a phenomenon much discussed in social and political circles.

3.3 Administration

Japan is divided into

47 prefectures;
43 rural prefectures (*ken*);
2 urban prefectures (*fu*), which include Kyoto and Osaka;
the capital city Tokyo (*to*); and
the island territory Hokkaido (*do*).

Furthermore, the prefectures are divided into

urban districts (*shi*)
small urban districts (*cho*) and
rural districts (*son*).

The directly elected prefect represents the interests of the prefecture to the central government in Tokyo.

Japan is a member of the United Nations, but does not have a permanent seat on the Security Council. It also belongs to the World Trade Organization (WTO) and the Organization for Economic Co-operation and Development (OECD), to name just the most important of Japan's many international commitments.

3.4 Social structure

Population growth

On 1 October 2003 the Japanese population numbered 127.6 million, of which 62.3 million were men and 65.3 million women. Population growth in 2003 was 0.14 per cent annually. Amongst the industrial nations, Japan has the longest life expectancy; at the same time, the birth rate is only 9.3 per cent (births per thousand people); on an average each Japanese woman gives birth to only 1.29 children (Table 3.1). Japan is already the country with the oldest population

Table 3.1   Life expectancy in various industrial nations

	Year	Male	Female
Japan	2001	78.1	84.9
Sweden	1999	77.1	81.9
Switzerland	1999	76.8	82.5
Germany	2001	74.4	80.6
Australia	1999	76.2	81.8
The Netherlands	1999	75.3	80.5
France	1998	74.8	82.4
USA	1998	73.8	79.5

Source: Facts and Figures of Japan 2004, Foreign Press Centre Japan, p. 10.

in the world. The high percentage of old people is already the subject of numerous discussions about how to safeguard pensions and health systems in the future.

Until the mid-20th century, Japanese households characteristically were made up of three generations sharing their lives and living quarters. Rising prosperity, deliberate family planning and increased life expectancy are in the main being made responsible for the breakdown of these traditional structures. Currently, the impression is one of old people having to manage on their own. New ways of living in new types of accommodation after retirement are developing (Conrad and Saaler 2001). In June 2002 there were around 46 million households, an increase of 12.8 per cent compared to 1995, a much faster rate of increase than that of the population. It is not young people but the elderly who are in single households. The proportion of these has risen considerably since the mid-1980s and now represents 23.5 per cent of all households (Table 3.2).

Today, the most frequently encountered family structure in Japan is the nuclear family. The average age at marriage is

- 27 for Japanese women and
- 29 for Japanese men.

According to official statistics, most of the Japanese population belong to the middle class. This is also in line with the way the Japanese see themselves: 90 per cent of them assign themselves to the middle class, even though their standard of living often looks

Table 3.2 Changes to household structures (in per cent)

Household	1970	1990	2002
Single	18.5	21.0	23.5
Nuclear family	57.0	60.0	60.3
Single parent with child(ren)	5.1	5.1	6.2
Married, no children	10.7	16.6	21.5
Married with child(ren)	41.2	38.2	32.5
Three generation household	19.2	13.5	10.0
Other	5.3	5.6	6.3

Source: Ministry of Public Management, Home Affairs, Posts and Telecommunications, Nihon tokei geppo, January 2004.

different in reality. However, the differences between rich and poor are not so pronounced as in other Western industrial nations. Status and hierarchy are accorded considerable importance and are given ritual expression by the appropriate symbols on the consumer market. The newest model of anything on the market is ideal (car, mobile phone, digital camera, fashion and so on).

The Japanese do not give an unambiguous answer to questions about their religion: many Japanese consider themselves Buddhists, but at the same time are members of the Shinto faith. However, Shinto ("the path of the gods") is more than a religion; it is a cultural expression of a sense of community and national identity. Shinto arose from a simple reverence for nature, and is genuinely Japanese – only the Japanese are Shintoist from birth. It is not possible to convert to Shintoism. Christianity plays a minor role in Japan.

Where the Japanese live

Most Japanese nuclear families live in their own house. The average living space per person of $29.9\,m^2$ is still slightly less than in Germany ($38.4\,m^2$). Overall, however, the living space for each living unit at $89.59\,m^2$ is even slightly more than in Germany ($84\,m^2$) and can be explained by the wide regional differences between the densely populated areas and other areas. Around 44 per cent of the total population live in the three largest urban areas around Tokyo, Osaka and Nagoya (figures for 2000), and 78 per cent of Japanese live in cities (Conrad and Saaler 2001).

The high cost of rent and property is one of the reasons why Japan is by a considerable margin the most expensive country in the world. Prices in Tokyo and Osaka are around 40 per cent higher than in New York and even much higher than in major European cities.

Foreign managers who relocate to Japan for some years have access to a separate property market which meets US requirements regarding generously proportioned space and the way it is arranged. Special estate agents find living quarters for the expatriates who have an appropriate budget to allow them to pay the high price of the expensive living space in the conurbations.

Tip

Looking for somewhere to live in the conurbations

Foreign managers should plan to spend some weeks looking for an apartment or a house in the Japanese conurbations, as the location of the living quarters is as important as the age and the fittings and furnishings. Houses older than 15 years should be avoided, as the Japanese method of lightweight construction means that they often do not meet up-to-date standards of hygiene, structural engineering and earthquake protection. Good public transport links should be a prerequisite.

Roles

The roles of men and women are more clearly delineated in Japan than in many Western industrial countries. Traditionally, the man is the breadwinner, whilst his wife takes care of the household, bringing up the children and taking care of the family's social life (relatives, friends, neighbourhood and so on). Most unmarried women work and have to give up their career after their marriage (Shire 2003). When they return to the labour market, they are usually accommodated in casual and part-time jobs. Both before and after marriage, women must be content with much lower incomes than men. Whilst women can run their households relatively independently and alone, their career options are still, even today, relatively limited.

Tip

Use neglected resources

In traditional Japanese companies, female newcomers are usually given only administrative duties (making tea, photocopying and so on). They are seldom given responsible jobs and are often excluded from important decision-making. Foreign companies could exploit a source of expertise so far neglected by Japanese companies if they offer ambitious and well-qualified Japanese women the opportunity to develop their careers.

Combining family, household, job and child raising, which is highly competitive, represents a constant challenge and a strain to many Japanese women. Stronger personalities who reject the system of social values and expectations often become outsiders, an idea which many Japanese women shrink from.

Only a few women dare to take the step towards independence and set up their own business. If this step, which attracts much social pressure, is successful, the women are accepted by the rest of the business world and do not suffer from gender discrimination.

Working life and life in general for men remain largely separate from that of women until the man retires, so the result is not infrequently marital crises and divorce when the man, whose time was previously monopolized by his company, starts to play a less minor role in family life. The world of men is more or less congruent with the world of work. Travel time of two hours is not rare in the Tokyo and Osaka conurbations. Most commuters prefer not to use their own car, due to the traffic conditions and limited opportunities for parking in the inner cities. The suburban public transport system is perfectly configured for commuter habits.

An obstacle

A cultural idiosyncrasy: The nap

In Japan it is generally acceptable to take a refreshing nap in public places (on the underground or in meetings and so on). At international conferences or meetings, however, this behaviour is met with amusement or even possibly distrust. Japanese business partners caught napping should not be assumed to be indifferent; rather it should be accepted as a cultural idiosyncrasy intended to improve concentration.

The constant career pressure experienced by male employees, for whom the Japanese word *sarariman* has been coined (made up from "salary" and "man"), can result in death from overwork, *karoshi*, a phenomenon which in recent years has been discussed publicly in society. The majority of younger Japanese are now saying that they are turning their backs on the work system and social ethics with which the older generation achieved the rapid reconstruction after the Second World War and the Japanese economic miracle. Family and leisure time have become more valuable to the younger generation.

Tip

At home and at work: Think hierarchies

Consideration and respect are key mainstays of the social structure of families in Japan. The younger family members address the old members with respect as a matter of course. The Japanese family is characterized by a hierarchical and not a lateral structure, similar to Japanese society. Japanese employees therefore see themselves in their position as part of a higher-level whole. Areas of responsibility are clearly demarcated and cannot be extended at short notice.

The world of work

Education is recognized as having a high, possibly the highest, importance. In Japanese society, education forms the basis for social advancement. From kindergarten onwards, through school and university, the different educational institutions act as both filters and catalysts and determine career and therefore also social advances.

The larger Japanese companies recruit their new staff from one of the country's elite universities (Tokyo, Kyoto, Keio or Waseda); the choice of university is often based on company tradition. After taking a difficult entrance examination, the students are under no more pressure to perform in their actual studies. They are mainly concerned with social skills, with the membership of university clubs and building up networks which will remain in place throughout their lives. In general, the rule is that graduates are moulded into shape after they enter the company by spending time in different departments. The requirement is for generalists and the development of versatile strengths that can be deployed anywhere and not for specialists. Therefore Japanese employees joining a foreign company always require quite a long introductory period even at management level.

An Obstacle

Japanese managers

Foreign companies often search in vain for Japanese managers who can be deployed internationally and not just in Japan. Expatriates are still appointed to key functions (such as CFO and CEO) in foreign companies for this and other reasons. Where Japanese senior managers are deployed, they generally have several years' experience of working abroad. English has prevailed as the business language in most foreign companies.

Average annual working time is about 20 per cent higher in Japan than in Germany. This is essentially due to much shorter annual leave. Most employees now have an entitlement to around 15 days' leave per year, but it is traditional for Japanese employees to expect that only a few days are taken of these three to four weeks (Haak 2005). Furthermore, the normal 8-hour day usually extends for several hours in the evening. After this overtime, which is not compensated, the meetings often continue at the company's expense in a relaxed atmosphere in a restaurant or bar close to the office.

Tip

International companies are considered attractive

Salaries of Japanese employees of European companies tend to be higher than those usually paid by Japanese companies: the reason for this was the supposedly less favourable image of foreign companies. Surveys indicate that there is currently a shift in thinking and Japanese employees are beginning to appreciate the benefits of foreign companies (all annual leave can be taken, more international, better social conditions generally).

Traditional Japanese features in the area of Human Resources (rigid salary systems, working times, hierarchies) are still considered very important, but are giving way more and more to international standards and allowing employees more individual responsibility and entrepreneurial thinking (Vaubel and Höffinger 2003).

Traditional Features
strong identification with a company and therefore lifelong employment in this company;

pay based on age and length of time in the company (seniority principle);

company benefits, which extend into activities and issues outside of the workplace (holiday, home, sport and leisure facilities and so on).

Changes towards international standards
more flexibility in drawing up work contracts (part-time work, short-term contracts);

performance-based pay (for example, a bonus for knowledge of foreign languages);

higher starter salaries for younger staff, particularly in future-oriented sectors like IT (company benefits extending to the private sphere are becoming obsolete) (Haak, U. 2001c).

4
Japanese Management

For 20 now, Japanese production management has been the subject of lively interest and debate in the West. Particularly the 1980s and the early 1990s saw a real boom in the publication of scientific writings and works of popular science which tried to get to discover the secret of Japanese success. One of the best-known papers is the study carried out by the Massachusetts Institute of Technology (MIT) researchers Womack, Jones and Ross in 1990, which intrigued whole legions of production scientists, management researchers and industry practitioners and had a key impact on subsequent research and on the Western view of Japanese production management and also on the self-image of Japanese production management itself.

In the course of the International Motor Vehicle Program (IMVP) the MIT researchers highlighted the differences between the factories in the automobile industry worldwide. They derived from the data of this study the basic hallmarks of the production system that became known globally as Lean Production and with which Japanese production management in the automobile industry, particularly the Toyota Production System (TPS), is equated.

The MIT researchers posited the theory that Lean Production would change the world in the same way as Fordist mass production had in the past, so that sooner or later all the important automobile manufacturers would be forced to adopt the Japanese system. However, the existence of "one best way" revealed itself as a myth during the 1990s. A number of Japanese automobile manufacturers, once paradigms of Japanese production management, were forced to enter into partnerships with foreign counterparts; in some cases, the management of the company was also handed over to ensure continued competitiveness. Others, however, such as Toyota and Honda, were able to maintain their worldwide leadership and continued to develop their specific forms of production management. Toyota's profits increased every year and it now occupies second place in the world ranking behind GM and ahead of Ford.

In order to examine Japanese production management one must first of all ask what is meant by production management, the development and nature of which will be analysed in the following pages. In this chapter, production management is meant as the management of manufacturing companies. This interpretation is based on the integrative approach to production management where production management includes the running of production processes, quality management, logistics, maintenance, industrial engineering and procurement.

The TPS, which is so essential for understanding Japanese production management, can be seen as a technology-based, comprehensive production management system with the primary goals of increasing productivity and reducing costs (Monden 1983). This is achieved by reducing cycle time, increasing flexibility, reducing stock levels and shortening machine changeover times. The difference between the concepts of Lean Production and the TPS is that Lean Production (Jürgens 1994) was coined by the MIT researchers Womack, Jones and Ross and is used for any company in any branch of industry, whereas the term TPS refers to the production management system at Toyota, but includes basically the same elements. Liker gives us an impression of what exactly is a lean enterprise in his latest book *The Toyota Way* (2004). "You could say it's the end result of applying the Toyota Production System to all areas of your business. In their excellent book, Lean Thinking, James Womack and Daniel Jones define lean manufacturing as a five-step process: defining customer value, defining the value stream, making it 'flow', 'pulling' from the customer back, and striving for excellence. To be a lean manufacturer requires a way of thinking that focuses on making the product flow through value-adding processes without interruption (one-piece flow), a 'pull' system that cascades back from customer demand by replenishing only what the next operation takes away at short intervals, and a culture in which everyone is striving continuously to improve" (Liker 2004, p. 7).

This chapter cannot discuss all the aspects of production management mentioned here in the same detail. It is more important to highlight key developments, identify change and continuity in production management and illustrate the particular characteristics of Japanese production management. Special attention will be paid to the TPS as it has made its mark permanently on Japanese production management. However, one should not make the mistake of thinking that the TPS is simply identical to Japanese production management. There are different forms of production systems in Japanese companies which also vary depending on the industry sector. Two central issues for discussion in this chapter arise from these preliminary observations. On the one hand, we examine the question of which central factors have influenced the development of the key features of Japanese production management; in other words, where were its roots, where were the important factors shaping Japanese production management, particularly in its most striking form, Toyotism?

Secondly, we look at the issue of whether the strength of Japanese production management, as expressed, for example, in the TPS, derives from its nature as a dynamic rather than as a static system, from the fact that constant change is inherent in the Japanese production management system, forming the basis for a flexibility which ensures that the system can survive in the face of rapidly changing competition and market constellations. In other words, can the Japanese production system be understood as a key factor in the corporate processes of learning, adaptation and improvement, as the key factor in a learning organization? Are change and continuity the main characteristics of the Japanese production system?

4.1 The early years

A look back at the development of production management in Japanese companies reveals that the global successes of Japanese companies over recent decades can be linked in no small part to technology and knowledge transfer and the associated advances in organizational learning. One of the areas in which the success of Japanese production management crystallized was automation technology and, following on from that, the development of the autonomation system (*jidoka*) at Toyota which will be examined in greater detail later. Successful transfer and further development of advanced automation technologies from the United States and Western Europe were important prerequisites for the emergence of a specifically Japanese system of production management and also therefore for the unstoppable economic and technological advance of Japanese manufacturing companies following the Second World War.

The organizational learning processes that took place in Japanese manufacturing companies as the result of technology and knowledge transfer changed their organizational and management structures and their competitiveness forever. The development and widespread use in Japan of the automation technology which came with the new forms of production and technology management and a specific form of work organization were crucial to the rapid rise of Japanese companies in the decades after 1945.

Adopting and improving technology from the United States and Western Europe, increasing productivity with new forms of work organization, management and staff development together with automation technology, a nationwide programme to improve quality based on the thinking of the Americans Deming and Juran coupled with a high degree of flexibility were the key elements that enabled Japanese companies to catch up quickly with advances in organizational learning. With many Japanese companies integrated in networks in which many different sectors came together (*keiretsu*), it was possible for learning the advances made in automation technology, quality management systems and production management to disseminate.

On an individual level, it was the commitment and willingness to learn on the part of Japanese technicians, engineers and managers, particularly those in companies engaged in electro technology, mechanical engineering and machine tool building and in laboratories undertaking research into manufacturing science which made the advances in production management possible. Toyota's key role in this process will be examined in greater detail below. Improving the existing situation and implementing the findings in practical applications characterize the development of production management in Japanese companies.

Along with the transfer of technology and knowledge, it was the industrial integration of innovative automation technology and new forms of work organization and company leadership which characterized the production management of successful Japanese companies.

4.2   Progress

We have seen that Japanese production management following the Second World War, particularly during the economic upturn since the 1950s, was determined by advances in the automation of factory operation. The use of innovative automation technology in changing production processes made a lasting impression on the work of production management. The rapid economic boom in Japanese industry paved the way for a systematic transition from automated single- or special-purpose machines to automation of the entire manufacturing process. Learning processes from the level of the individual up to the whole organization made it possible for the changes to take place in Japanese production management, which was working on ever newer and better solutions to increase the competitiveness of products and the efficiency of production processes (*kaizen*). The change in production management was linked to the economic boom in Japan. Indeed, each was possible by the other.

The years of reconstruction

Immediately after the Second World War, Japan became involved in building up and shaping new economic structures (Freedman 1988). From the economic and technological point of view the reconstruction of the country's economy took centre stage (Itô 1992). Shortly after the war, price controls, subsidies and allocation of resources were some of the most important tools of industrial policy with which the government supported and promoted coal and steel production.

The most important factor in Japan's rapid economic development was the meteoric industrial boom which lasted into the early 1970s (Tsuruta 1988, p. 50). At its core were mass production, automation technology and the specific nature of Japanese production management (Park 1975; Nakamura 1996). The reforms which took place during the time of the American occupation were also important for the dynamic development of the Japanese economy (Waldenberger

1994, p. 23). The deconcentration measures took effect in disentangling the threads of capital, organization and personnel that bound together the ten big business conglomerates (*zaibatsu*), thus creating the conditions for the competition which fuelled the reconstruction and high growth phases up in the beginning of the 1970s (Beason and Weinstein 1994).

Furthermore, foreign demand for Japanese goods stimulated and accelerated economic development in the early 1950s (Abegglen and Stalk 1985). The development of Japanese industry was further shaped by a dramatic event in world politics when the Korean War broke out on 25 June 1950, which, with the tense situation engendered by the Cold War, resulted in an increase in demand worldwide. Particularly, the extensive contracts with the United States had a marked effect on Japanese mechanical engineering. This boom in demand contributed to the recovery and stabilization of the Japanese economy which at the beginning of the 1950s was still weak (Itô 1992, p. 11).

After a short phase following the Korean boom in which the growth rate slowed, due mainly to falling private capital investment, the period of the so-called "investment boom" began in 1956–57 bringing *kôdo seichô* (rapid growth). Large amounts of investment were directed at the development of heavy industry. It was intended to increase production capacity and drive on modernization and rationalization of production facilities. Economic policy was set to growth (Chalmers 1986). Production management was looking for solutions to meet the increased demands on production output, production quality and processing quality. The advances made in quality management by researchers and managers in the United States were adopted and underwent target-oriented development in Japanese industrial operations.

Between 1955 and 1960 real growth in Japan was at 8.6 per cent – annual growth rates of GDP in terms of per cent – from 1960–65 it was at 10.6 per cent and from 1965–70 it peaked at an astounding average of 11.2 per cent (Itô 1992, p. 45; Keizai Kikakuchô 1994, pp. 46–7). Even though the period of high growth in the Japanese economy until the first oil crisis in 1973–74 was not without fluctuations, expansion in the 1960s was astonishing, given the extent of the destruction suffered in the course of the Second World War (Hemmert and Lützeler 1994, pp. 23–44).

Key industrial sectors

Up to the 1950s, the branches dominating in the processing industry were those which had also reigned prior to the war – the textile industry, for example. However, along with the primary industries, the assembly industries also developed into mainstays of the high-growth phase (Waldenberger 1996). These included automobile construction, electrotechnology, mechanical engineering, particularly machine tool building, and precision engineering (Nakamura 1996).

These branches of industry presented a particular challenge to automation technology and production management and were the drives of changes in the Japanese production management. It was important to coordinate the individual manufacturing stages effectively and efficiently and at the same time achieve low unit costs and high standards of quality. It was in these sectors that the innovative forms of Japanese production management had the most lasting effect, with the automobile industry in the vanguard. The development of the TPS played a key role here.

Dialogue was taking place between national and international researchers into manufacturing science and production economics and between industrial practitioners. As a result, the automobile industry and its supplier companies, in particular machine tool construction for process technology, became both the vehicle and the engine of Japanese efforts to develop automation (Spur 1991, p. 16) and of production management with its aim to make companies more competitive. The fundamental learning and transformation processes which made possible the successful introduction of automation technology and new forms of production management took place in the assembly industries, with the automobile and electronics industries in the lead. The use of technology and new ways of organizing labour and production processes were mutually dependent. Changes and continuity in the Japanese production management can be seen especially in the use of technology, the ways of organizing labour (work organization) and the various production processes.

Advances in learning and knowledge in science and industry

Advances in learning and knowledge in manufacturing technology and production management in Japanese companies in key industries were reinforced by the Japanese state, which encouraged the learning process with technology and knowledge transfer from abroad. It promoted existing and new branches of industry with tax breaks and by granting cheap loans. Foreign currency was allocated specifically for importing raw materials and advanced machine technology. International exchange of scientists was supported by the state so that new knowledge could disseminate throughout the different levels of industrial production management via universities, scientific organizations and, last but not least, the organizations themselves. All this allowed knowledge of quality management to spread quickly throughout Japan with the deep impact of the change of Japanese production management.

In addition to all this, the domestic market was closed to imports and direct investment. On the one hand, this was to protect emerging domestic industry and its specific models for organizing production processes, and on the other, to facilitate the import of technology because it reduced the ways in which foreign companies could enter the Japanese market to technology licensing (Waldenberger 1998, p. 47).

The new knowledge of innovative manufacturing technology and forms of production process organization was disseminated rapidly throughout a company. This was done in the form of quality circles, for example, which were the basis and instrument of organizational learning processes in Japanese companies. The quality circles moved learning processes and knowledge from the individual level onto a broad organizational basis. The members of the organization share the same knowledge about the production management of their company and use methods they have worked out together to develop the existing pool of knowledge – a key requirement for organizational learning processes in production management (Ducan and Weiss 1979; Garratt 1990; Geißler 1996; Hanft 1996).

During the economic boom years, investment in Japanese industry was used primarily for rationalizing and modernizing production facilities, presenting challenges to management which had to adapt to constantly changing manufacturing processes (Nihon Kôsaku Kikai Kôgyôkai 1982, pp. 81–3). This can be regarded as an evolutionary process in the development of production management, which was given essential impetus by innovation in manufacturing technology and by the changes and opportunities in the work organization with which it interacted.

The machine tool industry

One sector, as central supplier to the assembly industries, had a key role in the development and performance of manufacturing technology and hence also for production management: machine tool building. As the supplier of production resources the machine tool industry provided the technological basis for development for other areas. Hence, the Japanese automobile industry profited in particular from the technological innovations in the machine tool sector; in other words, from the advances in learning in this area (Takayama 1997). These advances were apparent in the artefacts of learning, the precision-automated machine tools and the associated forms of production organization in automobile manufacture.

Competition-oriented deployment of innovative machine tool technology was one of the main tasks entrusted to production management. Since the evolutionary development process of production management came from this key industrial sector – machine tools – we will take a closer look at this area in order to gain better understanding of the developmental forces behind Japanese production management.

Immediately after the Second World War, impetus for growth in the Japanese machine tool industry came largely from domestic industry, as did specific technological requirements relating to production. It was not until later at the start of the 1970s that Western European and American companies gradually began to make up large groups of customers for Japanese machine tools (Collis 1988). However, first of all, in the 1950s and 1960s, it was necessary to close the gaps in basic technology by importing advanced machine tools. Technology and management knowledge were bought in and adapted to Japanese manufacturing requirements.

However, it was not only a matter of company-specific learning processes in order to master new manufacturing processes. It was particularly important to pass on the production knowledge and specific forms of production management to suppliers to enable them as quickly as possible to achieve the level of knowledge required to develop the advanced technology and new forms of production organization. This was learning through technology and knowledge transfer as a type of "wet nursing". It was provided by the key production companies in the conglomerates (*keiretsu*) to the under-developed companies supplying the Japanese mechanical engineering, automobile and electronics industry in the 1950s and 1960s and represents an extended form of organizational learning in production management.

New learning processes – Innovations in production technology

One of the most important stimuli for tackling new learning processes, frequently associated with the establishment of innovations in production technology for machine tool building, was the increasing demand for machine tools generated by the development of the Japanese economy. The import of very modern machine tool technology, particularly from Western Europe and the United States, close cooperation between Japanese machine tool businesses and their suppliers, and long-term collaboration with universities researching manufacturing science provided Japanese machine tool builders at the end of the 1960s and beginning of the 1970s with the technological and scientific basis to meet increased demands from the national and international markets (Fischer 1979).

Due to the economic conditions prevailing in those years, attempts at automation using conventional machine tools concentrated mainly on applications in large series and mass production. Japanese production management focussed its endeavours on automating the manufacturing process. Automation, particularly for the users of machine tools, above all in the automobile industry, was driven by the development and widespread use of the modular construction system (Spur 1979) during the economic boom with its enormous demand.

Flow lines – Artefacts of organizational knowledge

Flow lines were groups of several, mostly highly productive, special-purpose machines linked together according to the flow principle and in which several manufacturing procedures were carried out in one station with automated workpiece handling. These flow lines of machines represent artefacts of organizational learning. This change in automatic manufacturing equipment was associated with organizational learning processes. The organization learns and changes in the course of the learning process its technological arte-facts (tacit knowledge) so that it can react appropriately to internal (for example, employee training) or external (for example, market demand) challenges.

In the 1950s and early 1960s Japanese industry was initially domi-nated by rigidly linked manufacturing machines. This arrangement was characterized by the automatic transport of the workpiece by feed systems with a shared control system in a cycle time which was determined by the longest work cycle (Chokki 1986). Fixed flow lines were used primarily in the car industry with its large unit numbers of each workpiece. Crankshafts and camshafts, valves, stub axles and transmission housing, to name but a few examples, were produced on fixed flow lines at this time.

Electronic control systems, which formed the crucial element of a transfer line (Kennedy 1954; Griffin 1955), have been used since the late 1950s, meaning that the development of flow lines also depended on advances in the electronics industry. Technological innovations on the part of Japanese machine tool suppliers became a dominant influence on the technological status of the machine tools and production management. The fundamental element of any flow line was the control system which became the subject of extensive research and learning by American, Western European and Japanese engineers (Spur 1991, p. 498).

Flexible flow lines

The technological realization of fixed and later flexible flow lines (Adler 1988, p. 36) was supported and made possible by the rapidly developing supplier industry which was given important impetus in Japan by the special forms of the *keiretsu*. In Japan, innovative impetus for further development of automation technology came from the area of electrotechnology (Asanuma 1989). With the use of machine tools in automatic flow lines, the main job of the control system was to repeat the same series of movements quickly and with precision so that mass-produced products were created with con-sistent quality without any human intervention in the production process (Mommertz 1981). The automatic manufacturing process was provided by a control system adapted to the technical production conditions in question, with a distinction made between mechanical, electrical, pneumatic or hydraulic control system components.

Controlling the machines

Whereas the introduction and widening use of machine flow lines was dependent on the demands of mass and large series production, Numerical Control (NC) of machine tools in the late 1950s and 1960s was used mainly for made-to-order or small series production. Previously, mechanical, electrical and hydraulic copy control systems with templates as fixed programme media had been used in this kind of production. The influence of NC technology on machine tool building in Japan resulted in just a few years in completely new types of machine. Designers and production engineers were asked for new design solutions. Numerical control technology which had a fundamental impact on the development of machine tool technology became the engine of the whole production technology system (Simon 1969).

Management of production technology systems faced increasing challenges which paralleled the technological development. Japanese scientists and managers sought solutions to improve the quality of both the products and the manufacturing processes. Developments in the United States concerning both the technology and the management thinking also lent impetus to the specifically Japanese forms of production management.

Numerically controlled machines – A leap in innovation for production technology and work organization

As we have seen, the beginnings of computer-controlled automated manufacture can be traced back to the development of numerically controlled machine tools in the United States. The NC system as a successful innovation and fundamental technological paradigm goes back to the digital machine tool control system devised by Parsons and developed with the MIT (Kief 1991). The basic idea of controlling a machine tool with numbers, that is numerical control, developed in association with the manufacture of rotor blades (Hirsch-Kreinsen 1989, 1993; Spur 1991).

The development in the United States and later in Japan of numerical machine control systems based mainly on rapidly developing computer technology and electronics has been crucial in shaping Japanese industrial production since the late 1960s (Behrendt 1982, p. 19; Park 1985). The learning processes did not only happen on a national level. Japan was dependent on international involvement in production technology research in order to ensure that organizational learning processes took place in production management via knowledge and technology transfer. The technological concept of NC became known in Japan for the first time in 1952. At that time, Professor Akira Takahashi from Tokyo University reported on the development of numerically controlled machine tools in the United States. A short time later, intensive research in this new area of production technology started in Japanese machine tool businesses, in the electronics industry and at universities and state-run institutions. The first result from these joint efforts was a revolving hole punch machine launched by Fujitsu in 1956 (Hoffmann 1990).

More developments in NC technology followed in rapid succession. As early as 1957, the Tokyo Institute of Technology announced the completion of a numerically controlled lathe for experiments and further investigation. Soon after, the machine tool manufacturer Makino Milling Machine developed the first Japanese vertical milling machine with NC in cooperation with Fujitsu.

Science, industry and bureaucracy as coordinated catalysts in the development of production technology

In the early stages of Japanese NC technology, the numerically controlled lathes from the company Ikegai and a jig borer designed by the Mechanical Engineering Laboratory at the Ministry of International Trade and Industry (MITI) (now the Ministry of Economy, Trade and Industry (METI)), as part of a three-year research project, represented further important steps forward. In 1958 Hitachi Seiki designed a hydraulic numerically controlled milling machine, also in cooperation with Fujitsu, two of which were supplied to the Heavy Industries Nagoya Aircraft Plant (Hitachi Seki 1991, p. 16).

Although the Japanese manufacturers of numerically controlled machine tools still had to struggle with high development costs and serious quality problems at the beginning of the 1960s, the trend reversed at the end of the decade. Market resistance was gradually overcome, demand for flexible manufacturing technology grew rapidly and the Japanese and then later the American and West European markets became receptive to numerically controlled machine tools from Japan. Technicians, engineers and production managers in Japanese machine tool businesses and research establishments realized their advances in learning from knowledge and technology transfer in stand-alone products. It was these products that underpinned Japan's outstanding competitive position on the world markets in the 1970s and 1980s.

One of the key advances in learning and knowledge for the Japanese NC machine industry was the development of the electrical and electrohydraulic stepper motor by Fujitsu and FANUC (Fujitsu Automatic Numerical Control) (Schröder 1995). The great advantage of stepper motors compared to conventional drive technology is that they allow the design of more precise, more reliable, more powerful but primarily comparatively cheaper numerically controlled machines. These could also be manufactured in larger series and accounted to a great extent for the huge success enjoyed by the Japanese machine tool industry (Brödner 1991). However, it was not only in drive technology, which is all-important for production, that the Japanese engineers became so proficient so rapidly. They also caught up with American and Western European development in control system design. Between 1965 and 1969, Japanese machine tool businesses launched the first NC control systems with integrated minicomputers (Spur 1991).

The rise of FANUC can be seen as an example of the Japanese success story in the time line of automation technology. FANUC started life in 1972, hived off from its parent company Fujitsu. Fujitsu played a significant part in the development and distribution of NC technology in Japan. As early as 1956, as a consequence of a strategic decision by the Fujitsu management, the company was concentrating on computers and control systems. The company began to encourage long-term development in production technology which became financially successful only ten years later.

The idea of developing an NC control system at Fujitsu was propagated primarily by Dr Seiuemon Inaba, who also played a key role in its execution. The development of the control system presented Inaba's research and development team with a considerable number of technical problems, the first being the construction of computer circuitry. However, after ten years of development, they succeeded in producing a low-cost, efficient NC system. The FANUC 260 for point-to-point position and linear path control was coupled to three electrohydraulic motors. The launch at the end of the 1960s in Japan triggered a considerable sales boom (Spur and Specht 1990; Schröder 1995, p. 147).

Flexibilizing and decentralizing production processes

In the late 1960s and early 1970s, Japanese research and development concentrated mainly on application research and on putting the new NC technology to use in the processing industries. The first numerically controlled machines were deployed in mechanical engineering, automobile production and the electronics industry. However, it was only with growing experience and advances in problem-solving and learning processes that Japan's own discoveries of new technologies became important for production technology in Japanese companies.

Technology and knowledge transfer from Western Europe and the United States as the object and catalyst of individual and organizational learning processes in the early years of automation technology was implemented in many different ways. The Japanese mechanical engineering industry within the framework of collective strategies made intensive use of the opportunity to acquire patents and licenses and to enter into co-operation agreements with leading technology companies in the mechanical engineering sector and the electronics industry (Nonaka 1990).

Working together with European and American businesses not only facilitated technology transfer, but also made it easier for Japanese companies to enter foreign markets. Integrating Japanese scientists and engineers in international research into manufacturing technology was also crucial for the advances in organizational learning brought about by technology and knowledge transfer. To all intents and purposes, Japanese management and engineers fared well with cooperative ventures. As cooperative strategies coincided with structures receptive to learning, they represented the crucial factor for successful technological and economic development in Japanese industry following the Second World War.

Using CNC systems – New impetus for production management

The use of Computer Numerical Control (CNC) systems had far-reaching consequences for the options for designing manufacturing processes. The organization learnt and modified the structures that it needed to fulfil the tasks. The use of these new CNC systems made it possible for preparatory work on the manufacturing process to be removed from production planning and returned to the worker and the actual place of production. On the basis of this vastly important development in technology, demands to abandon the division of labour increased. Japanese production management was forced to react. The aim of these efforts was to reduce division of labour from "as much as possible" in accordance with Taylor's principles to "as much as is required" in future. The work process was to be carried out by employees who were as highly qualified as possible and with full content and wide-ranging autonomy.

Japanese businesses were very receptive to NC and CNC technology. It is interesting to note here that in Japanese companies, as compared with European companies, the requirement for advanced and continuing training associated with the introduction of the new NC technology in manufacturing processes represented only a small obstacle. One reason for this was that manufacturers of control systems and machines ran intensive training and support programmes when NC was first developed. Customer employees were trained and supported for over six months. Particularly in the introductory phase, engineers from the manufacturers were on hand to guide customers through the first application steps and to help with troubleshooting.

Furthermore, when entering on their career with a company, Japanese manufacturing engineers were first employed in processing, where they frequently became highly qualified at user level (Koshiro 1994, pp. 247–9). When a new employee was taken on, the part of the company in which he/she would work was not at that point clearly specified. He/she needed to be flexible enough to change direction in the company (staff rotation), as he/she needed to absorb new information and learn new accomplishments and skills. This is primarily individual learning in order to cope with new challenges in working in the company. Staff rotation takes place in formal management systems and tried and tested bureaucratic structures. This form of learning is a long way from organizational learning unless the employee shares the knowledge he/she has acquired in the previous position with the new group (participative learning) and, according to Ducan and Weiss (1979), creates a basic prerequisite for organizational learning – developing a knowledge base shared with other members of the organization.

New forms of work system design

Since the mid-1960s, the impact of automation, computer technology (NC and CNC technology), flexibilization and decentralization of manufacturing processes has led to a fundamental change in the way industrial businesses work and in individual and organizational learning processes. Japanese production management has also undergone radical changes. The new forms of operation which became more important in Japanese industry at that time were those which aimed to reduce the functional division of work by integrating tasks (Spur 1994, p. 217).

With computer support in the factory, particularly with the use of CNC machines, there have been new opportunities for work system design since the end of the 1970s and beginning of the 1980s. It became possible to establish different forms and varieties of group work as rational alternative forms of organizing labour in Japanese factories, or to be more precise in automated manufacturing processes, with the wider use of computer-assisted manufacturing equipment. Technological changes and individual and organizational learning processes have been mutually dependent. Job enlargement, job enrichment and change of job location could be realized simultaneously as a principle of design as illustrated by the development of the TPS.

Production management at Toyota – The Toyota Production System (TPS)

The TPS, which combines advanced automation technology and forms of organization, is an expression of both learning through technology and knowledge and the process of continuous improvement of structures and systems referred to as the corporate philosophy of kaizen. The term "Toyotism", which is heard frequently in the context of discussions about Japanese production management and which is equated with the TPS, has established itself mostly as the opposite, but sometimes as an extension of or complement to "Western Taylorism" and "Fordism" in scientific discussion and in industrial practice.

Similarly to Fordism, the TPS is used mainly in large companies which have concentrated on mass production. The distinguishing feature of Toyotism is Lean Production (Clark, Fujimoto and Stotko 1992; Jung 1992; Boesenberg and Metzen 1993; Scherm and Bischoff 1994; Freyssenet, Shimizu and Volpato 1998; Durand, Stewart and Castillo 1999; Liker 2004; Haak 2005). The economic success enjoyed by many Japanese manufacturing companies in the 1970s and 1980s introduced the concept of Lean Production in the 1990s, which is frequently seen as the antithesis to Fordism, to mass production as practised in the West.

Alongside these two central basic concepts of Fordism and Toyotism, there are many different peculiarities and specific ideas in Japanese production management which reveal themselves in the different ways in which technology is implemented, in the organization of production management and in the self-image of Japanese industry. In the following, I will present and discuss the most important basic concepts and forms of organization including production management at Toyota and Toyotism, as TPS had a considerable impact on the development of production management in Japan itself. Nevertheless, it should not be assumed that the manifestation of production management at Toyota is that of the whole of Japan, even though Toyotism has made a deep impression on the form of production management in other industrial sectors.

A discussion of the work system design issue

Engineers and managers at Toyota were not the first to apply themselves to the question of how to organize work systems in the production process. There have been many scientific examinations of work systems design issues, particularly that of work organization since the mid-19th century. However, the findings by economic and production scientists and by managers with an interest in the design of work systems had a considerable impact on the form and implementation of production management at Toyota.

In other words, to understand the development and the current production management situation at Toyota and from that to understand the key elements of Japanese production management, it is necessary to review the defining concepts of production organization. We must also consider manual production, Taylorism and Fordism, which influenced the shape of Toyotism. Despite all the reservations regarding simplification of this kind, it is first necessary to sketch out an outline of the organization of production, both to highlight the necessity of a differentiated view and also to illustrate the main influences on the TPS. It is not sufficient to fall back on the study by Womack, Jones and Ross although with its international comparison it made a key contribution to the understanding of the special productive capability of the TPS and opened up a perspective of the specifics of Japanese production management via the concept of Lean Production in the Western world.

Demands on qualifications – Craft production ability versus mass production

The high demands made on the capabilities, skills and knowledge of production employees at Toyota are major features of the production system, aimed at achieving maximum flexibility on the part of the employees. This approach comes from the way production was organized for manual production of single units which prevailed before the Industrial Revolution. Manual production was primarily geared towards the work of a single worker, in many cases a craftsman (master, journeyman, apprentice, unskilled labourer), on whose capabilities and skills high demands were made.

This form of manufacturing was characterized by single-unit production and low-unit volume achieved with simple and very flexible tools. It allowed customer requirements to be met on an individual basis. The major disadvantages of this form of organization are high costs, limited volume, little potential for a progressive reduction in unit costs and the possibility that the quality of the product might fluctuate wildly.

Mass production on the other hand makes little demand on the qualifications of the workers in the production process so that fluctuations in quality due to individual performance are more of an exception. To complement the workers with few qualifications, many well-trained specialists (for example, manufacturing engineers) were deployed. Manufacturing was characterized by the use of special-purpose machines which processed standardized and precision-made parts. The use of machines increased the amount of fixed capital so that management was at pains to achieve high utilization.

The key advantages of this form of organization compared to manual production are high production capacity, low unit costs and much potential for a progressive reduction in unit costs. The key disadvantages are its lack of flexibility in responding to changes to the production programme and the high proportion of fixed costs. The beginnings of this production system, known today as Fordism, can be found in the 19th century. Charles Babbage (1791–1871), to pick a name, is representative of the many practitioners and scientists of the early rationalization movement which went ahead of the American "rationalizers" and is also considered the father of modern factory development.

It is to Babbage's credit that he recognized the contradiction between the potential offered by manufacturing technology on the one hand and the limited efficiency of a workshop organization rooted in tradition on the other. He concentrated on analysing and applying the principle of functional division of labour. By formulating the goal of organizing an operation scientifically, he crossed the threshold to a new, systematically thought-out organization of the production process. An intellectual thread links Babbage to Frederick Winslow Taylor (1856–1915).

Taylorism

Taylor applied the ideas illustrated by Adam Smith's (1723–90) examples of production processes in the pin factory. He developed methods for analysing work processes and breaking them down into the smallest possible task elements to be completed by different workers. He recorded his ideas in two major works *Shop Management* (1903) and *The Principles of Scientific Management* (1911).

Like Babbage, Taylor recognized that in the transition to larger companies and to mass production, the rationalization of businesses remained very much underdeveloped compared to the manufacturing technology. His response to this was to require that companies made what happened in them more transparent and that production procedures were better planned, and to afford work more consideration as a factor in production. This challenge has been met consistently by the Japanese rationalizers since the 1950s. The unstoppable advance of the Japanese quality management system, as illustrated so impressively in the Japanese automobile industry, has its roots in Taylor's challenges to corporate production organization.

Scientific principles for the organization of production

The significance of exact coordination of production capacity and production times was discovered early on. Even craft workshops were not able to do well without preparing their work at least mentally. However, with manufacturing processes becoming very complex, Taylor demanded the institution of business management based on scientific principles, which would become the subject of a specific scientific discipline – the science of management, later manufacturing science.

Taylor's *Principles of Scientific Management* supplied the name for a new way of management thinking which was characterized by the rational deployment of humans and machines in the production process, with maximum output oriented towards the most efficient worker, appropriate personnel selection and incentive systems and consistent separation of operational and planning activities. Accordingly, Scientific Management not only meant the systematic study of methods and time (Industrial Engineering), but also included the results of the new thinking on efficiency. This is a line of thought which has been continued through the American production line system and Japanese Toyotism into the present day.

Taylor's division of labour led to a relative reduction in the number of workers physically engaged in a specific stage of production, as the time-consuming mental and creative work was concentrated into a single function. The precise allocation of predetermined tasks together with the specification of rules regarding minimum quantities and times and detailed work routines meant that every single step in the work process and in the execution of the work was controlled. Control, in the sense of discipline and monitoring, became the most important management task besides work planning.

There were more economic benefits besides the gains in productivity associated with division of labour. A company could buy the qualifications required for such an organized production process in the form of an unskilled labour force. This came much more cheaply than the traditionally integrated and therefore highly qualified and highly paid skilled worker.

Time studies – Avoidance of waste

Frank B. Gilbreth (1868–1924), one of Taylor's most prominent students, complemented his time studies with movement studies of the work flow. He believed that any movement that was not of immediate benefit to the production process meant that time was being wasted. Specific work organization was supposed to rid human work of all irrationality and chance and all unnecessary abilities and skills. Together with Henry L. Gantt (1861–1919) and Carl G. L. Barth (1860–1939), Gilbreth is considered the founder of a new area of research known as Industrial Engineering. This area of research was characterized by increased technical support of the time and movement studies.

In the search for the most useful methods of factory rationalization, Taylor and the influential school of Scientific Management which he had founded were faced with powerful competition in the form of the ideas and practical successes of Henry Ford (1863–1947). Particularly, following the end of the First World War, Ford became the new role model for America in technology and organization. Henry Ford published an account of his experiences in designing the production processes in his factories in his book *My Life and Work* (1922).

Fordism – Effective rationalization with the reduction of waste

Whilst Taylor was still primarily concerned with rationalizing physical, mainly manual, work, Ford concentrated on rationalizing the industrial manufacturing process for mass production. The rationalization strategy known as "Fordism" was characterized first and foremost by an optimum arrangement of humans and machines engaged in the assembly of uniformly mass-produced objects. It reduced considerably the amount of working and transport time wasted. Ford followed the principles of increased typification of products, high production mechanization (line production) and aptitude testing to select the best workers. With the low levels of education prevailing at the time, Ford was forced to keep the operational activities of the production process as simple as possible. Ford had two goals: precise division of labour and production line working.

It is obvious that Fordism was based on the experiences of Taylorism in the implementation of manufacturing using production technology but the two production principles should not be considered equivalent. Taylor can be considered a theorist for breaking down manual work in the more or less pre-mechanized phase of industrial production, whereas Ford, as a successful industrial practitioner, realized mechanized mass production with the production line system. With his new concept of a flow of materials using a conveyor belt, he revolutionized the product-manufacturing methods familiar at that time. Initially, in this way of organizing production, individual workers moved from one assembly station to the next to carry out their tasks. Later on, the conveyor belt transported the work to the workers. However, this new form of production organization required completely interchangeable and precision made parts and simple assembly. Accordingly, the same measurement principle was used in the whole production process.

The principles of production according to Ford

The Fordist production principle was also characterized by high manufacturing penetration and associated self-sourcing, which meant that everything had to be produced with as few bought-in parts as possible. In order to break even with this form of production organization, mass production according to Ford had to reach a high production volume to achieve a low price with the associated progressive reduction in unit cost and increasing profitability. Ford's products had a very long market cycle, which is linked to these factors.

Characteristic of conveyor belt production, this new phase of development in manufacturing technology was a rigid automation which due to the large amount of time and effort taken by set-up and changeover had to produce large unit volumes in order to run economically. Mechanically controlled production machines proved highly productive. Synchronized lines of machine flow shops, transfer lines and special-purpose machines with extensive division of labour led to single-purpose machines with high-volume output and low manufacturing costs. Further development of fixed automation became apparent in a step-wise transition from automated single-tool machines to automated process sequence of linked machines.

Transfer lines

The use of transfer lines obviates the need for industry workers to physically transport products and, to some extent, the need to control the transport procedures in mass production. More staff were assigned to work on planning and quality control in order to carry out planning, checking and monitoring operations during the production process. The development of fixed automation was the most important production form in the 1960s and in some sectors has retained its significance for mass production to this day. The American automobile industry worked primarily with transfer lines, which were referred to as Detroit automation after the place where production was highest. It was only with Toyotism's "triumphal march" that a new successful production type became widespread in America and Western Europe. Discussions about the Japanese success in automobile production have long included a search for explanations for this. The explanations range from the powerful Japanese automation through easy-to-assemble products to culture-specific attributes.

The factory as a whole system

The TPS has made its mark on industrial practice and on manufacturing science research in places other than in Japan. It embodies in Lean Production a corporate approach and a basic company strategy that view the factory as a whole system, as a work system overlaying the single workstation and the workshop. Essentially, Toyotism concerns the developmental mainstays of production management: manufacturing technology and work organization. It tries, whilst avoiding any form of waste, to combine the benefits of manual production – Taylor's central interest in rationalization – with the advantages of mass production (Fordism).

As Toyotism became more widespread, internal and external production logistics (just-in-time) took up a key position for corporate success along with work organization and manufacturing technology (autonomation, *jidoka* in Japanese). Toyota people usually explain just-in-time and *jidoka* as the twin pillars of the TPS (Nihon Noritsu Kyokai 1978; Ohno 1978; Monden 1983) and do not highlight the work organization system specifically, although it plays a large part in the success of the TPS.

The term *jidoka* can be translated as autonomation. This term includes, on the one hand, the concept of automation and, on the other, that of autonomous monitoring for defects and elimination of their causes. In automated work processes, a defect or poor quality can cause the machines to come to an immediate standstill. Work can continue only when the cause of the problem has been removed. If one work stage is interrupted, the whole production system can come to a stop as the constraints of kanban allow only minimum interim stocks. In some cases there are no interim or buffer stocks. Therefore the production workers have to be in a position to find the defect as soon as possible and take the appropriate steps towards fixing it to minimize production down time. For example, all the workplaces are supplied with light indicators called *andon* to call the workers allocated to that particular production section to help. The potential for disruption to the production system resulting from autonoma- tion, quality assurance and cost reduction has also earned Toyotism the name "Management by Stress" (Parker and Slaughter 1988). Fur- thermore, social pressure on less-productive employees in the group can cause problems for the productivity and motivation of the group members. From the point of view of the learning organization, that is looking at autonomation from the aspect of learning theory, stress within a certain context (taking into account intensity, time period, constitution of the individual, social norms) can, however, promote learning.

Lean Production was developed for the manufacture of passenger cars in the Toyota Motor Company's factories and is used pri- marily in the automobile and the automobile supply industry. It did not remain limited to Japan: it has proved to be an effec- tive structure for production in other economies and achieved considerable productivity and quality effects (Schmitt 1998; Yui 1999).

The Lean Production approach originated with Eiji Toyoda and Taiichi Ohno. In a well-known study by the MIT, which was pub- lished in 1990 under the title *The Machine that Changed the World*, Toyota's factors for success are named as technology leadership, cost leadership and time leadership.

In their comparative study, the authors find the main factor for success in Japanese companies is a different system of production from that practised in European and American companies: Lean Production. In their view, Lean Production combines the advantages of manual production with those of mass production, whilst avoiding the high costs of the former and the inflexibility of the latter. On the one hand, many multiskilled workers work in groups, as is the case in manual production; on the other, large volumes of standardized parts are produced with the aid of flexible automated machinery – similarly to mass production (Womack, Jones and Ross 1990).

The findings of the international comparison made in this study between mass and Lean Production are summarized in the following list of Lean Production features:

– fewer defects in automobile manufacture;
– the manufacturing process is much faster;
– the repair area in the company is smaller;
– the stocks held by the company are smaller;
– the majority of employees work in teams;
– the workers frequently change their job within the company in the production area;
– the workers offer more suggestions and are trained for longer;
– the organizational structures are flatter.

Essentially, the key factor is organizational learning, which manifests itself as the result of the advances in manufacturing technology and in work organization, improved product quality and careful use of resources. Other features of this organizational learning system are low warehouse stocks, shorter product development times, low staffing levels and, especially at Toyota, involvement of assembly workers in the permanent quality control system and the continuous process of improvement (kaizen) (Shimizu 1988). As a result, production errors fell dramatically and costly post-processing was minimized.

Kaizen

Kaizen can be interpreted as the Japanese management philosophy which involves every employee in achieving the goal of continuous improvement of structures and systems (Hayashi 1991; Jürgens 1991). The starting point for this philosophy is the knowledge that each business is confronted with many problems which can be solved by establishing a company culture with two main features: each employee can with impunity point out errors and identify problems, and solutions for the weaknesses identified are found by the employees of the organization working together (Imai 1993; Yamashiro 1997).

Continuous improvement of structures and systems uses a systematic procedure based on Deming's PDCA cycle (*P*lan, *D*o, *C*heck, *A*ct). The PDCA cycle is used in Japanese companies to initiate, track and review improvements. Approaching the matter systematically, the cycle begins with the *p*lan phase (Liker 2004, p. 24). For example, the area earmarked for improvement is discussed in the work group and the most important findings and the biggest obstacles are identified. Then the current situation is analysed. In order to proceed efficiently, the problem under investigation is defined and described precisely. To identify causes, relevant data is collected from the production workers. A quantitative base of data is indispensable for identifying clearly the potential for improvement and defining appropriate interim goals and actions. This is also a requirement for making the targeted improvements unmistakably visible to all the employees in the course of the improvement process.

In the *d*o phase of the improvement cycle, the actions selected are carried out. This does not mean, however, that it is impossible to return to the plan phase if necessary, in order to gather more information and review the actions. Defining the actions is only the first step on the way to achieving the improvement of the production systems and structures.

In the *c*heck phase that follows, the effects of the planned actions are analysed. An investigation is carried out into whether and how the goals defined in the planning phase can be achieved. The results are monitored, documented and illustrated in the activity catalogue. Regular monitoring reveals whether the goals have been achieved. If this is not the case, then investigations are carried out into why the undesirable deviations occurred. Even failures hold important information for shaping the improvement process.

The last phase of the cycle – *a*ct – serves to review the previous phases and to record the experiences made during the process, by standardizing successful factors and making them obligatory for other employees in the company, and to initiate follow-up activities, from which targets for subsequent improvements can be set up. If the cycle is carried out sequentially as it is intended to be, the problems under consideration are increasingly limited as knowledge and experiences from the previous cycles can be applied.

The newly created standards or rules set up by the *kacho* or *bucho* (in some Japanese companies by the *kakaricho* or *kumicho*) as results are not set in stone. The aim of the standard is not only to create a basis for further improvement, but also to encourage confidence in consistent quality, to create a solid basis for worker education and training and to remove product liability problems (Suzuki 1994). The old standard is replaced only when a new one is defined in the course of the improvement process. The role of the *kakaricho* or the *kumicho*, the immediate supervisor, who does not work in production with the other employees, is to find new templates for standards on the basis of the daily production data and to push through improvement measures together with expert kaizen teams, who are assembled specifically for the problem situations, or with work groups. The PDCA cycles running on the different levels of the company can be integrated both upwards and downwards in the hierarchy. This creates multifunctional project teams primarily in the area of product development or in production process innovation. Problems which cannot be dealt with on one level of the company or in a functional area are referred to the next highest level or to a level with the specific subject knowledge, as are faults in the production process, so that precisely the knowledge required for solving the problem can be applied. In this context, the integrated PDCA cycle can also be understood as a process of organizational learning in which subject knowledge and experience can be gathered on an individual basis and made available through the improved standards to be worked with throughout the company.

Avoiding waste

A central concern of kaizen is to eliminate or avoid waste of all kinds in the company. Frequently, waste in a company is not perceived because it is associated with processes that have developed historically and new, simpler options are not even considered. Seven areas with the potential for waste have been identified in the production area:

(1) The most important area is overproduction, where a larger volume is manufactured than is required by the internal or the external customer. Unnecessary process stages are created with this kind of waste with serious consequences, as over-production in its turn can cause a number of different types of waste. The just-in-time system developed by Toyota and product control with the kanban system have provided a remedy to this situation.

(2) Overproduction leads to more work-in-progress. This represents waste as it requires space, incurs storage costs, requires to be searched, makes additional movement of materials necessary and, above all, conceals problems in the production process (for example, machine downtime) or unstable processes.

(3) Also, any form of transport is classified as waste in the TPS, as material transport does not in itself add value. Workstations placed at a distance from each other result in additional costs for the transport of work-in-progress. The turnaround time of the product or the workpiece is longer, thus increasing the job time calculated for the manufacturing process.

(4) One outcome of big buffer inventories and lengthy transport are waiting and idle periods.

(5) This form of waste results in an unbalanced utilization of workers and machines. Waste in the manufacturing process is frequently a result of the previously listed types of waste. However, there is also waste in the manufacturing process if there is a simpler or faster way to carry out a certain production task. This waste is caused by ambiguous instructions, lack of ability, skill or knowledge on the part of the employees or by too many unnecessary inspections.

(6) One of the basic premises of kaizen, that the manufacturing process can always be improved, is that unnecessary motion should be avoided, by reducing the number of movements in the work flow by changing the work systems (for example, avoiding long distances, repeated refamiliarization due to too many unnecessary interruptions).

(7) Defects, the seventh waste area, arise frequently due to inattention or lack of concentration. Defects in their turn also cause other

kinds of waste, such as repetition of work, or long idle or waiting times.

Employees – The source of improvement

One of the basic convictions of kaizen is that nobody knows a workstation as well as the employee who works there in the production process day in, day out. For this reason, the aim of kaizen and hence the Lean Production philosophy as embodied by the TPS is to increase productivity and employee motivation by eliminating waste within the framework of a systematic and consistent operation.

How should waste be eliminated from the work environment? This is one of the central issues of kaizen and therefore one of the fundamental issues for Japanese production management. In other words, how can the knowledge, the experience, the skills and the expertise of the workers be used to create the most effective work system? The 5 S process can be applied to the whole company or focussed on just one workstation. The core of the 5 S process to combat waste can be understood as follows:

1 S (*seiri*): The employee needs to decide which tools and accessories are required at the workstation.

2 S (*seiton*): The employee needs to put the tools and accessories he/she thinks he/she requires in order so that they are at hand in the right place at the right time when he/she needs them for his/her work.

3 S (*seiso*): The employee needs to keep the workstation clean; that is, clean and take care of the orderly workstation and the tools and accessories.

4 S (*seiketsu*): The employee must observe standards, rules and regulations; he/she must turn instructions into rules.

5 S (*shitsuke*): The employee must observe all the points listed and improve on them continuously.

The 5 S process is not a fashionable trend in management science. It originated in the Japanese manufacturing industry and forms a central part of Japanese production management. One can posit the theory that the 5 S process forms part of the self-image of a Japanese production manager in any industry sector. The central question from a business management point of view is, what are the benefits of continuously maintaining and improving the work environment? The answer is quite simple: it creates more time for the value-added process, or time can be better utilized.

Tools for solving problems

Through kaizen, tools have been developed for solving problems which are intended to enable continuous improvement in the interests of the customer. Quality assurance, just-in-time, automation, extensive product monitoring, kanban, suggestion schemes and much more are linked together under the kaizen "umbrella" (Sebestyén 1994; Nonaka and Takeuchi 1997). First and foremost, kaizen encourages process-oriented thinking, as it is mainly corporate processes that are to be improved to allow goals to be reached more efficiently (Matzky 1994). Following Argyris and Schön (1999), this process-oriented thinking is equivalent to organizational learning. Implementation of the kaizen philosophy and its tools places the organization in a problematic situation. For example, the employees in a multifunctional project group (Hyodo 1987) find after systematic investigation that there is a discrepancy between the results they expect from their actions and the actual outcome of the actions. The employees examine the matter and try to rearrange their activities so that their actions and results are again congruent (Nonaka and Takeuchi 1997). Following Argyris and Schön's concept of the learning organization, the organization members' theory-in-use is modified if the discoveries leading to the solution of the problem are fixed in company-specific artefacts such as a change in the manufacturing organization and in new work programmes. The result of these modifications is that the organization has learnt (Argyris and Schön 1999).

A key element of this problem-solving process specified in the kaizen philosophy which can find negative deviations (performance gaps) is repeated analysis of an existing set of facts (Nonaka and Takeuchi 1997). Looking at the company to find the causes of problems and the reasons for performance gaps and identifying solutions is the core thinking behind kaizen. Continuous improvement of the processes means that all the members of the company are constantly learning so that they can, on the one hand, react flexibly to permanently changing challenges and, on the other, improve on the existing situation more and more. Kaizen is quite different from traditional methods of business rationalization as it is not a matter of large-scale innovation but of small, but continuous improvement.

Working in groups

In order to diffuse the philosophy of continuous improvement further throughout the company, product teams on the level of work organization and personnel management were put together under the leadership of Taiichi Ohno. In these product teams, each member was able to carry out all the stages in production. The group members were supposed to distribute the work in the group themselves and discuss and agree with each other on the ways to optimize the production process (Hyodo 1987; Nonaka and Takeuchi 1997; Ernst 1999).

Group work organization was seen above all as communication and dialogue to improve the group members' performance. Rotation within the jobs allocated to the group played a key role in employee training. The rotation plans were compiled on a daily basis by the supervisor and planned to allow weaker group members to improve their skills and to make provision for more effective employees to be on standby for when production was disrupted.

This form of work organization has cost-cutting (avoidance of waste) and productivity increase as its foremost goals; employee training is seen as the tool to achieve the goals. Training group members is important in planning for and working with a workforce that is as flexible as possible. However, note here that there are groups of employees (such as short-term workers, new recruits or employees from other areas) who are not considered for participation in these job-rotation schemes. It also takes some time before work experience is sufficient to allow group members to be included in the rotation scheme.

The existing training and problem-solving potential of employees deployed in the context of wide-ranging improvement activities also form a key source of information for creating adaptable work systems. The structural integration and harnessing of individual knowledge gained through experience is a comprehensive programme which runs on all levels of the company. For production, these are quality circles, suggestion schemes and improvement measures at the individual worker level. All these activities are supported by work groups, teams of experts or individuals.

The just-in-time system

On a concrete level – the flow of parts in the production process – Ohno developed the well-known just-in-time system, which is represented in the literature in many different and occasionally contradictory ways. The determining features are group technology, the kanban system, short set-up times, harmonization of the production process and quality assurance (Görgens 1994, p. 15).

This astonishingly simple and economically so promising idea was that in each stage of the process only as many parts are produced as necessary to cover the immediate requirements of the next manufacturing stage. Empty containers are returned to the previous processing stage which is the automatic signal to produce more parts (Ohno 1978; Shimizu 1988). Essentially, this just-in-time system is oriented towards intra-company and inter-company processes. A just-in-time system would not be thinkable without the conscious implementation of collective strategies in the organization. Toyota undertook to guarantee its suppliers a certain volume of orders over a certain period and furthermore was prepared to share with them the profits achieved with the cost savings if the partner adopted the TPS – in this particular case the just-in-time principle of pulled material flow.

Teams of design and production engineers

Another modification to work organization which affected the whole production process at Toyota was the grouping together of design and manufacturing engineers in teams and the encouragement given to group-based success. Learning and knowledge boundaries within the organization were abandoned and the knowledge available on different hierarchical levels and the associated methods for solving problems were put on a broader plane. As a result of this change to work organization, development time for new car models fell dramatically and product quality again improved. This structural change also represented a considerable advantage from the marketing policy point of view. It was possible to respond more quickly to changes in customer requirements and penetrate a number of niche markets intensively and at a low cost.

Organizing a team as an independent and accountable business unit initiates learning where performance gaps are identified and makes knowledge available so that team members can carry out their work. Each team member has the ability to carry out many, in some cases different, types of work within the group and the resulting redundancy creates a very flexible company (Hyodo 1987). With shared knowledge bases, organization as a team forms the basis and is a catalyst for organizational learning in Japanese companies (Ducan and Weiss 1979).

Quality management

In Japanese manufacturing companies, quality is at the centre of the product and process-oriented efforts towards improvement and innovation integrated in the kaizen company philosophy. Economic success comes only when the customer is convinced of the quality of the product. The high quality of Japanese products and the quality management systems in Japanese businesses are considered exemplary today.

Originally the development of production-oriented quality procedures derives from American ideas and industrial applications (Deming circle and quality control). The process of continuous improvement is based on the PDCA cycle which was developed in the 1950s by W. Edwards Deming, an American. Following the Second World War, these American "achievements" were methodically developed into Total Quality Control (TQC) in Japan and then developed further into the Total Quality Management (TQM) of today. Quality circles are a central core element of the total quality management system (Goetsch and Davis 2003). These quality circles, which are held regularly and are supported by engineers can also be seen as a central element of the learning organization as they identify performance gaps and lead to a review of the way the organization works.

Before the Second World War, the emphasis in Japan was on (final) inspection, which, in line with Taylorism, was carried out by a dedicated quality control department. American influence after the Second World War brought about the introduction of statistical quality control (1946). The modern Japanese concept of quality circles therefore has its roots in the period shortly after the Second World War. The year 1946 saw the foundation of the Japanese Union of Scientists and Engineers (JUSE), which promoted the development of quality control in Japanese manufacturing businesses considerably. In the 1950s, on the initiative of the JUSE the idea of systematic quality assurance was brought into Japan.

It was American quality experts who shaped the eventually independent quality system in Japan. In the years 1950–52 Deming held a series of lectures on the subject of "Statistical quality control" (inspection during production). Joseph M. Juran emphasized in his seminars (1954) the role that top and middle management should play in quality control. Armand V. Feigenbaum, who invented the term TQC, extended responsibility for quality to all areas of the company. Quality no longer meant the elimination of defective products but that they were avoided from the beginning by monitoring the process. These methods were developed further in Japan. One of the most important representatives of the Japanese movement was Kaoru Ishikawa, who extended quality management to include social aspects. Another step forward was taken by Masaaki Imai, who postulated that continuous improvement of processes to raise the standard of all output would be a recipe for success in Japanese quality management.

These efforts resulted in the first official registration of a quality circle in 1962. At the beginning of its development, the quality circle was a learning group which then gradually evolved to solve problems with practical application of techniques it had learnt. Japanese production management moved further and further away from traditional inspection-oriented quality control and developed quality procedures for use within the production process and within product development.

Today, this idea is also applied to suppliers and other business partners who play their part in the value-added process. Whilst quality control originally focussed on production and other technical areas in the company, efforts are made far beyond that nowadays.

The core idea of the quality circle is that problems are most likely to be identified and eliminated whenever they occur. Using this approach, production employees are supposed to identify the weak points in their day-to-day work and find the solution themselves. The primary goal of the quality circle is to improve the quality of the product and the process.

Quality circles have two main aims:

1. to optimize manufacturing processes and work flow using the employees' knowledge and experience;
2. to improve job satisfaction and motivation with regular group meetings which also improve company-internal communications (knowledge transfer, exchange of experience, transparency).

Kaizen – Core of Japanese production management and embodiment of organizational learning

Organizational learning processes have been made possible by the transfer of knowledge and technology (for example, automation technology and the autonomation system at Toyota) and frequently form the basis for the development of systems (NC and CNC technology and manufacturing applications), which in their turn enable organizational learning by modifying the knowledge base (knowledge linked to the technology, for example manufacturing processes) in the organization.

Organizational learning in production through the company-wide and cross-company process of continuous improvement (kaizen) is one of the main characteristics of Japanese manufacturing companies, a key hallmark of Japanese production management. The endeavour to achieve a zero-fault strategy in Japanese production plants as part of the total quality management system, which means not only that a defective part is rejected but that the cause of the error is also removed, is an expression of kaizen and as such an expression of the fundamental thinking by Japanese production management.

In response to the technical problems with products and production which arose in the interplay between American, Western European and the Japanese methods and applications, the continuous improvement system today concentrates on production, but as a management concept includes all the activities and employees throughout the whole company. This means that Japanese production management can be considered as the management of the process of continuous improvement which forms the basis for the way manufacturing companies are run.

For instance, Japanese production workers, marketing experts and design engineers actively cooperate in groups to identify problems, find solutions and develop better technology in order to eliminate performance gaps they have identified. The improvements they work out apply not only to their particular working group but also become valid for other working groups via a central integration and coordination mechanism, for example works management.

The improvement becomes obligatory for all the members of the organization and also becomes a new standard and a long-term theory-in-use for employees new to the company. The search for improvements to products, processes and systems applies not only to the company itself, but as part of a collective strategy creates a bridge to inter-company cooperation (for example, involving supplier companies).

The high degree of standardization in the formal management systems of Japanese companies brings about successful learning in groups which benefits the whole organization; that is, it enables organizational learning. This knowledge is also passed on to or shared with other companies via the collective strategies (collaborating companies, value-added partnerships, alliances, supplier networks). New knowledge circulates through companies in the same networks very quickly. The highly regarded kaizen concept, the Japanese leadership philosophy which still remains valid even under the currently prevailing low-growth conditions, has proven to be an effective method for learning particularly in the area of production and enables progress in a combination of individual, organizational and inter-organizational learning.

Japanese production management is associated with specific forms of work organization (for example, group work, team organization), of logistics and quality (for example, just-in-time, kanban, quality circles), of manufacturing processes (high-tech manufacturing systems, NC and CNC systems, autonomation), of personnel deployment (for example, job rotation) and of education. Its main characteristic overall is that it has been strongly moulded by the TPS and is expressed in the philosophy of continuous improvement.

5

The Japanese Market: The Dynamics, the Potential, the Perspectives

5.1 The challenge to businesses

Goal-oriented exploration and penetration of the Japanese market, customer care, attention to business partners and to all the important local stakeholders in the company all present the management of a company engaged on an international level with great challenges. The Japanese market is considered one of the most demanding, but also counts as one of the most interesting and most profitable markets competing in the global arena. Nevertheless, small and medium-sized businesses are deterred from going into Japan. Frequently heard statements include the following:

- "You need plenty of ready money to get a business going in Japan."
- "Doing business in Japan is difficult because the Japanese have a different mentality and behave in an unusual way."
- "What they need above all are time, patience and a will of iron."

Empirical studies frequently refer to obstacles and problems which bedevil attempts to do business in Japan. The obstacles to doing business in Japan are as follows:

- insufficient market transparency and over-regulation
- economic stagnation
- highly intensive competition
- *keiretsu* structures (networks of companies)

- high costs (staff and rent in particular)
- tariff and non-tariff trade barriers
- multilayer sales system

Japanese managers are all too fond of using references to the positively mythological distinctiveness of the country compared to the rest of the world to reinforce this image of Japan held by foreign business people. They stress the close intermeshing of politics, business and ministerial bureaucracy (for example, Japan Inc.). The specifically Japanese business models with their groups, or networks, of companies (*keiretsu*) and their special Japanese supplier system are paraded as examples of Japan's exceptional position.

The Japanese also like to point to their special company and business culture which only the social and cultural conditions in Japan have allowed to flourish and which formed the basis for the success enjoyed by many Japanese companies after the Second World War (*nihonjinron*).

5.2 Governmental reform policies

The Japanese government has been working against this myth of a difficult and culturally unapproachable market for some time. Under the current reform policies, there are increased attempts to attract FDI. This could not be taken for granted in the past. Today, incentives are expected for

- management and business methods
- technology
- research and development
- innovative products and production methods and
- the labour market.

Foreign involvement should also contribute to the process of reform which the Head of the Government, Junichiro Koizumi, has been driving on since April 2001. Since the spring of 2003, efforts to attract foreign investors to Japan have increased. In June 2004, at the same time as the G8 summit in the United States, Koizumi himself advertised Japan as a location in the *Wall Street Journal* and on CNN.

He presented Japan as the gateway to Asia, as the region's centre of excellence with an exceptional infrastructure and well-qualified employees, and as a market with more than 120 million sophisticated consumers with plenty of buying power.

Since 1994 FDI in Japan has increased; particularly from 1997 to 2000, both the number of individual investments and their volume rose significantly. The global economy started recuperating after the slump in 2001 and 2002. However, it must be said that the overall increase in the second half of the 1990s took place at a low level. The value of FDI makes up only 1 per cent of Japanese GDP; for comparison, in 2001, direct investment in relation to the GDP of other countries was 24.2 per cent in Germany, 25.1 per cent in the United States, 32.2 per cent in China, 38.8 per cent in England and 42.8 per cent in France (DIHKJ & Roland Berger Strategy Consultants 2003).

The low volume of investment should not, however, lead to the conclusion that Japan is not a suitable country for direct investment, as the

- economic
- political
- social and
- institutional framework conditions

are extremely good. For foreign companies thinking about entering the market or penetrating further, the most interesting fact is that in recent years imports into Japan have increased more than exports out of Japan. Imports in the manufacturing sector increased by a quarter in the course of the 1990s (DIHKJ & Roland Berger Strategy Consultants 2003).

5.3   Market transparency and deregulation

The Japanese government is still concerned to increase market transparency and drive deregulation forward in the following areas:

- telecommunications and information technology
- pharmaceuticals
- medical equipment

- financial services and
- energy.

Foreign companies have frequently complained in the past about how difficult it is to deal with the complicated Japanese bureaucracy. Finding the right contact person for the matter in hand and getting the necessary information about business involvement, along with contradictory decisions on the part of various bureaucratic bodies and the amount of time and effort required, were among the familiar problems confronting foreign businesses.

To counter these problems and to increase transparency, the Invest Japan Business Support Centre (IBSC) was set up in May 2003. This is a part of the state-owned body for encouraging foreign trade, Japan External Trade Organisation (JETRO). Currently, JETRO maintains "Invest Japan Business Support Centers" in six cities from Tokyo to Osaka to Fukuoka which support potential investors with market and location information. If a foreign company decides to get involved in Japan, fully functional offices are made available to its employees for several months during the initial phase at no cost.

The IBSC has the task of bundling all the information on the subject of investment and making it available to foreign companies in English. The aim is to provide a better overview of the legal, economic and political framework conditions. Foreign companies should use this service at the beginning of their involvement for their market entry and market penetration strategies.

The JETRO also helps foreign companies to settle in Japan. It currently maintains a global network, with 38 offices in Japan and 74 in other countries, where companies can receive preliminary information and advice at no cost. There is a comprehensive service available to every company in Japan. JETRO's IBSC offers numerous cost-free services, not only to investors: English-speaking JETRO consultants, market experts and lawyers, tax advisors and so on hold surgeries in which they provide information about the steps needed to set up a company or develop a trading partnership.

The IBSC has contact points in every Japanese ministry, where questions regarding any aspect of investment can be answered quickly. It is also possible for representatives of foreign companies to use individual offices rent-free. This gives them a fixed address in Japan whilst they are searching for their own premises, with the

help of a real-estate agent found for them by JETRO, for example. The IBSC premises can also be used as an office whilst market
research is undertaken or as a meeting room. Secretarial services and
a library with business literature complete the facilities available.
In IBSC Tokyo, there is also a hall which can be used for product presentations or press conferences. The IBSC has a presence in
Tokyo, Yokohama, Nagoya, Osaka, Kobe and Fukuoka. In 2005 alone,
the IBSC helped over 400 foreign companies and oversaw over 100
successful company start-ups and other forms of direct investment.

5.4   The end of economic stagnation

Policies pursued in the years of the economic crisis (particularly during 1997–98 and 2001–02) were far from innovative. Observers at
home and abroad drew hope from the permanent reforms which
the LDP Premier Junichiro Koizumi promised when he took office
in April 2001. Indeed, following a downturn in economic growth in
2002 (the unemployment rate was at 5.4 per cent), government policy, increased exports and more corporate investment allowed Japan
to make up some economic ground in the years 2003 and 2004
(Bellmann and Haak 2005). At the beginning of 2005, unemployment
was at 4.8 per cent.

The economic growth figures reveal a trend that has not been seen
for years (Table 5.1). For the financial year 2004 (April 2004 to March
2005) the Japanese government is predicting a growth rate of around
3.5 per cent. However, for the fiscal 2005 (April 2005 to March 2006),
it is expected to weaken to around 1.2 per cent.

Table 5.1   Overall economic forecast (changes in per cent) by fiscal year

Indicator	2003	2004	2005
GDP	3.2	3–3.5	1.2–2.0
Private consumption	1.4	2.3–3.0	1.0–1.8
Private investment	12.2	9–10	3–5
Export	10.9	12–15	4–6
Import	4.9	8–10	2–4
Inflations rate	−0.2	−0.2	0–0.2

Source: Maurer (2005a, p. 7).

The boom is being driven by some higher investment from Japanese companies, but primarily by a good export performance on the part of the Japanese economy. Deliveries to the Peoples' Republic of China, the countries of Southeast Asia and the United States are the mainstays of this significant growth in exports.

However, the investment climate varies from sector to sector. Companies producing consumer electronics are finding plenty of opportunity for sales, and the demand in the IT market is driven by the modernization of the IT infrastructure carried out in many companies. The development in mechanical engineering is also positive as the manufacturing industry increases its investment in modern production equipment, and the demand from abroad is high.

There are many indications that economic growth will continue for the next few years. According to surveys, at the end of 2004 companies viewed the short-term prospects for the economy more positively than at any time since the beginning of the 1990s and consumers also saw much improvement in their economic situation, which consolidated urgently needed domestic demand.

5.5 Important markets

There are a number of very attractive growth markets in Japan which present promising prospects for market entry. There are opportunities in the following five sectors with high growth or potential for growth:

- Information and communications technology
- Automobile supply industry
- Environmental technology
- Medical and health technology and
- Biotechnology.

Furthermore, the Japanese government on national and prefecture levels is supporting companies who have established themselves in these areas and are encouraging the formation of clusters. Foreign companies also profit from these networks as parts of these clusters.

Information and communications technology

In 2001, the Japanese government set out their aim of making state-of-the-art Internet access widely available in the e-Japan strategy. The objective was to become the leading country in IT in the world by 2005. With the consequently wide coverage of broadband cabling and Internet connections, another target was formulated as early as 2004: the strategy was not just to cover IT infrastructure but also IT applications. The intention was to create by 2010 a "ubiquitous network society" called u-Japan in short (MIC 2005, pp. 5, 55).

High growth is expected in the coming years mainly in connection with the networking of information and communications media. Already today, Internet and wireless connections are used for numerous applications at home, for medical purposes and for paying for transport tickets by mobile phone, for example (JETRO 2005h, Internet and JETRO 2005i, Internet).

An increase in market volume is therefore expected for the following products and services: (radio) networks and IP telephony, devices such as PCs, network equipment, IC cards and so on, platforms (electronic authentication, security platforms, platforms for financial services) and services and content. Together with commerce (e-commerce, transactions with electronic tags and IC cards) and infrastructure (above all, corporate investment in hardware and software) studies are assuming that the market will triple in size between 2003 and 2010, with forecast growth rates in individual areas such as commerce, infrastructure, domestic networks and wireless networks far exceeding this estimate (JETRO and MRI 2005, pp. 8–9).

The governments of the Japanese prefectures are encouraging companies to settle in industrial clusters. For example, there are already numerous IT industry clusters. One of these is on the northern main island Hokkaido. Companies from the IT and mobile content industries have settled in the "Sapporo Valley", where they develop software for the leading mobile telephone company NTT DoCoMo (JETRO 2004c, Internet).

Automotive supply industry

Approximately 10 million cars are made annually in Japan; in 2003 this was around 17 per cent of the 61 million vehicles produced worldwide (JAMA 2005 Internet; JETRO 2005g, pp. 2, 4). Due to the high importance of the Japanese automobile industry, the largest foreign automotive supply companies, including numerous European firms, are already represented in Japan with their own sites.

As product development and design are carried out in close consultation with the customers, the vehicle manufacturers, a local base is essential in this sector. Furthermore, given the high demands of Japanese vehicle manufacturers, a presence in the Japanese market represents a seal of quality for many companies. The site in Japan often plays the role of regional head office for activities throughout the rest of Asia.

The times when Japanese vehicle manufacturers and their suppliers presented an impenetrable unit which left no opportunities for outside suppliers are over. Japanese vehicle manufacturers seek out the most reliable and most innovative business partners worldwide, taking into account technology, quality and cost. The example of the automotive industry illustrates cooperation on an international scale particularly clearly, with a strikingly high number of international joint ventures and share holdings (JETRO 2005g, pp. 70–71). A well-known and successful example is the shareholding of the French automobile manufacturer Renault S.A. in Nissan.

One of the regions particularly attractive for settlement by automotive suppliers is the Aichi prefecture or the area around Nagoya. The reason for this is mainly the presence of the Toyota headquarters and 12 of its production facilities in Aichi, amongst other companies. Many Japanese and foreign suppliers have set up here. Another important location for the automotive industry is the Fukuoka prefecture, where resident vehicle manufacturers include Nissan Motor Co. and Toyota Motor Kyushu (JETRO 2005b, p. 14).

Environmental technology

With the growing awareness of environmental problems and stricter environmental regulations, the Japanese market for environmental technology has grown strongly in recent years. The most attractive business areas include soil restoration, water treatment, fuel cells and renewable energies.

Japan is a densely populated country. Contaminated soil lowers the value of land and therefore has a direct impact on the property market. Investors who want to buy land are asking more and more frequently for proof that the soil is fully uncontaminated, so that the soil evaluation and restoration sector is becoming increasingly important. The Japanese government has reacted to these demands by passing the Soil Contamination Countermeasures Law (2003), which is intended to put pressure on those carrying out soil examination to do so without delay and to repair any damage. Accordingly there is a demand for methods to assess soil quality quickly and reliably, and for technology to clean soil polluted with harmful substances effectively and at the lowest possible cost (JETRO and JMA 2005, p. 66).

Water treatment is one of the large growth markets in Japan. Factories and production facilities which produce more than 50 cubic meters of waste water daily are subject to the Water Pollution Control Law. Technologies and plants for filtering nitrogen and phosphorus from the water are therefore in demand. Even smaller companies are subject to regional regulations which are often stricter than the national standards. Since 2002 it has been possible for private companies to act as operators of water filter plants. Since then, operators of sewage treatment plants have been forming Private Finance Initiatives (PFI) with private companies, which has also increased demand (JETRO 2004b, p. 14; JETRO and JMA 2005, p. 66).

Fuel cells can be used in a broad range of applications, of which the most important are undoubtedly the automotive industry and electrical household appliances, for example, for the bathroom and kitchen, and in underfloor heating. Numerous Japanese companies including Sanyo Electric Co., Panasonic and Idemitsu Kosan Co. Ltd., are researching fuel cells, and some household applications are already being tested. An example of international cooperation is the joint venture founded in 1998 between Ebara Corporation and the Canadian Ballard Power Systems Corp (JETRO and JMA 2005, pp. 70–71).

Japanese companies developing photovoltaic systems are amongst the most successful in the world. On the other hand, the Japanese market for wind energy is dominated by European manufacturers (Denmark, Germany and Spain in particular) (JETRO 2004b, pp. 38–40). Combined heat and power, biomass and biogas are also gaining ground.

The years since the end of the 1990s have seen the establishment of many environmental industry clusters and "eco-towns". The regions around Kawasaki and Kitakyushu are particularly well known on that score (JETRO 2005d, pp. 12–13).

Medicine and health technology

Not least due to the high life expectancy, the market for medical technology and health is one of the fastest growing in Japan. Life expectancy at birth is around 86 years for women and 79 years for men and is the highest in the world (figures from 2004, MHLW 2004, Internet). Furthermore, with the low birth rate, the proportion of elderly people in the population as a whole is growing. Just the "baby boomers" who will reach retirement age between 2007 and 2010 number approximately 10 million (JETRO and NRI 2005, pp. 1, 43). These and older people often have considerable savings and use them for their medical care and for wellness products, for example.

With this expectation of strong growth and high demand, the Japanese government supports foreign technologies and investment in this industry. Foreign companies new to the Japanese market are recommended to collaborate with Japanese partners in order to build on existing contacts with hospitals, health insurance companies and authorities and to apply for the required authorizations and tests jointly. Legislation was and is being appropriately adapted and deregulation is practised.

Some important changes that have taken place in recent years are listed as follows:

- The private sector is now also allowed to run medical institutions and care homes (JETRO and NRI 2005, p. 65).
- Medical facilities are allowed to extend their range with some services which are not covered by statutory health insurance. Until now, using these "free-care" services meant that all the costs for medical care had to be borne by the patient (JETRO and NRI 2005, p. 59).
- Reform of the Pharmaceutical Affairs Law (PAL) makes it easier to hive off medication manufacture (JETRO and NRI 2005, p. 62).
- Particularly the market for generic medicines profited from the 2002 revision of prescription fees. Its share has grown in recent years (JETRO and NRI 2005, pp. 34, 62).

The north Japanese city Sendai is one of the areas in which companies in the medical technology sector have settled successfully. In the Japanese–Finnish cooperative venture *Finnish Well-Being Centre* numerous companies from Sendai and Finland have joined forces to develop products and for reciprocal marketing.

Biotechnology

The Japanese market for biotechnology is the second largest in the world next to the United States, and in 2003 was worth approximately JPY 1.66 trillion (around EUR 12 billion). With the proportion of elderly people in the population overall on the increase and greater health consciousness, the Japanese Council for Biotechnology Strategies is assuming the market will grow to JPY 25 trillion (approximately EUR 188 billion) by 2010 and that most of the spending will be on medical care and health foods (JETRO 2005c, p. 4).

The Japanese government considers research and development in biotechnology very important. Money for research is preferably invested in basic research and in building up first-class research facilities. In order to drive on research in the private sector as well, 10–12 per cent of expenditure on R&D can be set against tax. Although this incentive does not apply only to biotechnology, it is considered particularly effective in this area as R & D costs are high compared to the turnover (JETRO 2005c, p. 6).

In order to support foreign companies setting up in Japan, parts of the Pharmaceutical Affairs Law have been changed, amongst other things. The registration formalities for manufacture and distribution have been simplified and combined to some extent, so that only a single licence is required for both. Furthermore, it is now permitted to outsource the manufacture of medicines to companies in Japan and abroad. Many of the other changes to the law affect protection of intellectual property, for example.

There are already biotechnology clusters in several regions of Japan. For example, in the *Kobe Medical Industry City* in the Kinki region (which includes the prefectures of Osaka, Hyogo and Nara), 52 firms and institutions conduct medical and biotechnological research, mainly for clinical applications and regenerative medicine. These include 13 foreign companies (as of January 2004, JETRO and Yano 2005, p. 170).

Kobe is also a "Special Zone for Structural Reform". In the course of deregulation, legislation governing statutory immigration and residence has been relaxed in these areas, so that ten more foreign scientists have been able to start researching in Kobe. There are more examples of successful biotech clusters in the Kanto region (Tokyo, and the Chiba and Kanagawsa prefectures with the city of Yokohama) and in the Nagoya conurbation (Aichi, Mie and Gifu prefectures) (JETRO 2004c, Internet and JETRO 2005j, Internet).

The Medical Valley in the Mie prefecture also maintains close scientific and economic links to the BioCon Valley in Mecklenburg-Vorpommern in Germany. This project was supported by JETRO in the Region-to-Region programme from 2003–06.

Trend – Aging society

Against the background of an aging society, Japanese companies have long been concentrating on the "silver market". Marketing is directed at older people, which here means the over-50s who have a lot of buying power and who want to continue to take an active part in society. These important consumer groups are targeted with product ranges in the following areas and clever marketing ensures that they enjoy great popularity.

- Body care and health
- Leisure
- Travel
- New Media (for example, mobile phones tailored to the requirements of older people)
- Financial services
- Real estate
- Job brokering

(Conrad and Gerling 2005).

Up to now, foreign companies have not had a presence in the market for older people but this segment is opening up enormous opportunities for them. Older Japanese people place a very high value on their international image; particularly, German culture and German products are highly regarded. JETRO is forecasting a growth of EUR 30 billion in 2002–07 in the market for senior citizens.

Of all the industrial countries, Japan currently has the fastest-aging population. The proportion of over-65s of the total population was 18.5 per cent in 2002. This has been forecast to rise significantly over the coming decades to 35.6 per cent in 2050. In absolute figures, the number of over-65s will increase from the current 23.6 million to 35.9 million, whilst the 15–64 age bracket will decrease over the same period from 85.7 million to 53.9 million (*Kokuritsu Shakai Hoshô Jinkô Mondai Kenkyûjo* 2004).

Furthermore, many retired households have hardly any debt and over 90 per cent live in their own property. Although some of their savings will be used to compensate for the relatively poor benefits provided by the public retirement pension or will be passed down as an inheritance, statistics nevertheless reveal that senior households in Japan have disposal savings relatively more freely compared to those in Germany. It is also doubtful that the previously held claim that older Japanese were anti-consumerist – and were therefore responsible for the long recession of the 1900s – is true. Since the mid-1980s, consumer spending by 60- to 64-year-olds has risen by 35 per cent and that of the over-65s by 40 per cent whilst the growth in spending by 35- to 39-year-olds has been 24–29 per cent.

As well as the purchasing power, the spending patterns of the retired population play an important role for tapping the "silver market". It should be noted that in principle there are no major differences from the younger members of the population. However, "health" and "culture and leisure" make up a larger proportion of the total household outgoings and therefore represent particularly interesting market potential.

Both the increasing significance of Japanese seniors in terms of numbers and the data on their financial clout and on their spending patterns illustrate that in Japan some of the major conditions for profitably tapping the senior market have been met.

In almost every area, from the body care and health market through the leisure sector, the new media and financial services to the property and job-brokering markets, there are interesting opportunities in the "silver market". The large marketing agencies have now noticed this and set up appropriate departments. For example, *Hakuhodo*, one of the pioneers in this segment, claim to make around 20 per cent of their turnover in this market. According to the company, three areas are particularly successful. These are the finance and insurance, travel, and automotive industries (Gerling and Conrad 2002).

In Japanese bureaucracy and politics, the negative sides of an aging society are no longer singled out for comment (the main concern being financibility of the social insurance systems), but there is now acknowledgement of the positive aspects of demographic change. For example, as early as 1997, the Japanese Ministry for Industry and Trade (MITI; now METI) identified the medical and charitable areas as the largest of 15 new growth markets. And 1.3 million new jobs are planned to be created here by 2010 (JETRO 2000, p. 6).

The following are particularly promising segments identifiable in the Japanese senior market: medical technology and care products for the elderly, technology for rehabilitation and gerontology, preventative medicine, Universal Design products (known as *kyoyô-hin* products in Japan), cosmetics and nutritional products (supplements and special diets), vehicles, new media (mobile telephones, PCs, Internet), hobby equipment, domestic appliances, home accessories, clothing, sports products, finance and insurance products and travel.

Examples of individual products that have enjoyed exceptional success due to innovative approaches to marketing to the older generation are as follows:

- Yoghurt products for older people from *Meiji* (LG 21; special bacteria for purifying the digestive system). These now have the largest market share in Japan (Interview, *Hakuhodo Inc.* 18.7.2002).
- The global cosmetics manufacturer *Shiseido* markets a product line for older people under the name *"Care Garden"*, which prevents the typical "old person's smell" (Interview, *Shiseido Co. Ltd.* 19.7.2002).
- The Japanese telephone company *NTT Docomo* promoted new media for older people in collaboration with *Hakuhodo*. Following the advertising campaign, the proportion of mobile phone users amongst elderly people rose from 27 per cent (1999) to 46 per cent (2001) (Interview, *Hakuhodo Inc.*18.7.2002).
- Building on the Japanese walking trend, which is mainly pursued by older people, various manufacturers have been developing walking shoes for the elderly since the 1980s. One example is the company *Tsuki Hoshi Kasei*, which brought this type of shoe onto

the market in 1987, and now offers walking accessories such as speedometers (Ley 2000).

For international suppliers, the opportunities are probably in those areas of the Japanese "silver market" where they are already relatively heavily involved, in the market for medical technology and care products, for example.

The development in care products in a wider sense, the *kyoyô-hin* products (literally meaning generally useful products), also deserves mention. These are characterized by their user-friendliness and their accessibility and are intended to meet the requirements of every group of the population (*Kyôyo-Hin* Foundation 2004; Yoshikazu 2002, p. 25). Since the mid-1990s, figures here show average annual growth of over 20 per cent (*Keizai Sangyôshô* 2002). Anyone entering the larger Japanese department stores will notice that these products are now advertised quite aggressively together with traditional care, health, nutritional and even design products. This represents an opportunity for Germany companies to build on a relatively strong position in the medical technology or care product market by diversifying into *Kyoyô-hin* products on the basis of the high regard in which German industrial design is held. Design-oriented care products such as high-quality wooden living room chairs with an integrated toilet (from Toto Ltd.) or stylish hospital beds (from Paramount Bed Co.) are enjoying increasing popularity.

As described above, the automobile sector should continue to be of interest to international companies. Almost every Japanese manufacturer now offers standard low-cost conversion solutions for people with physical disabilities. This will also be essential for German automotive companies in the future if they want to continue to be successful in Japan.

According to Japanese marketing experts the whole market for semi-professional hobby equipment also holds considerable potential for development. This includes products for golf, special sports articles for older people, artist's equipment, outdoor clothing and home accessories. If the Universal Design approach is taken more into account in product development in these consumer goods areas, it will certainly be possible to use the generally good reputation that the European design enjoys in Japan as a starting point.

Important marketing target group – Unmarried women over 30

Unmarried women over 30, who are mostly single and have an above-average income, are sophisticated and luxury-oriented consumers who also represent an important marketing target group. Known ironically as *makeinu* (bad losers) because earlier it was considered a disgrace to be over 30, childless and unmarried, this financially powerful group today confidently enjoys consuming brand products, buying their own places to live and travelling (Maurer 2005c).

Also of interest to market observers are the so-called "parasitic singles" who have grown up in relative affluence, have their own, usually high, income and are still financially supported by their parents (apartment, travel and so on) (Haak 2002b).

Lifestyle

The younger generations in Japan are extremely receptive to trends and innovative products. The keyword "lifestyle" is becoming increasingly important. Products or services which improve the quality of life, increase the value of leisure time and express individuality are very highly rated by the young Japanese. Interior design has gained significance in recent years and, as in many other areas, is heavily influenced by European and American lifestyle ideas. However, the combination of Western design with Japanese lifestyle plays an important role. Originality, comfort and making life easier are other important aspects in lifestyle marketing.

The enthusiasm shown by Japanese consumers not only for foreign input but also for emphasizing their own identity is illustrated by a look at 2004, the year in which the consumer goods market was characterized by three phenomena (Maurer 2005b):

- increase of imports of all kinds from South Korea (the Korea boom), prompted by a television series "Fuyu no Sonata" (Winter Sonata);
- increase in demand for home entertainment products (DVD recorders, plasma screens and so on) and for sport articles following the summer Olympic Games in Athens;
- high sales of goods which made Japanese tradition the core of their image campaigns ("Japaneseness"; for example, lemon-flavoured

green tea from Suntory or the "Asience" range of hair-care products from Kao).

Japan is considered ideal as a test market for new lifestyle trends. Having grown up absorbing new trends, the younger generations of Japan are fascinated by novelty value, and leisure pursuits and individuality are becoming more significant for them.

Lifestyle is not a product; nor is it a service. Nevertheless, it sells well. Lifestyle trends are dreamt up and implemented by designers and companies and made attractive to consumers by marketing specialists. Whether the consumerist Japanese follow these trends depends on their ideals and very much on the financial situation of the individual.

Japan as an experimental area for lifestyle innovations

Large Japanese cities, particularly Tokyo, probably have something to offer for every lifestyle from the vast range of goods and services available. A search with the keyword "lifestyle" reveals that there are 70–80 Japanese magazines dealing with the subject. They concentrate on categories such as fashion, food, interior design, cars and sport.

These are also areas which are heavily advertised. In the Japanese advertising market in 2003, shares of relevant products and services were 8.9 per cent for food, 6.9 per cent for cars and similar products, 4.2 per cent for hobbies and sport, and 2.7 per cent for clothing and fashion articles, according to figures provided by the largest Japanese advertising company Dentsu Inc. (2004). Lifestyle quite definitely has to do with improving the quality of life.

The young and the middle-aged have grown up in a time in which the quality of life has improved significantly and lifestyle cycles have become shorter. They like to try out new things, are open to new trends and ideas but, on the other hand, do not want to be seen as standing apart from their peer group, nor do they want to appear uniform. If it is at all possible to generalize about lifestyle, it is noticeable that in recent years the enjoyment of leisure pursuits and individuality have become more important, according to surveys by *Future Lifestyle Emphasis* (2003).

One Japanese company that recognizes these trends early and implements them in a technologically innovative form is, without a doubt, Sony, with its classic Walkman and the whole palette of new portable devices that have come onto the market since then. It could be said that the personal freedom of the consumer – freedom from the stationary hi-fi system at home – has undergone a quantum leap with miniaturization and portability. The company does justice to the individuality factor not only by making a large selection of models and applications available, but also by providing more and more options for its various digital products to be networked, allowing consumers to compile their own personalized content.

Multidimensional lifestyle

Lifestyle is not static, but is highly dynamic in Japan, making trend watching and trend changes fundamental for marketing. Even if trends change repeatedly, according to a study by the Japan Consumer Marketing Research Institute (2004), it is possible to differentiate between five key consumer types. A number of market research companies investigate the changing consumption patterns every year.

The Dentsu Centre for Consumer Studies (2003) found that 2003 was characterized by a more open, multidimensional lifestyle. After years of bad news about economic growth in Japan, it has seen the beginnings of a reversal which expresses itself in consumers' attitude and willingness to spend.

The Hakuhodo Consumer Trend Report (2003) also detected a change which manifested itself in a stronger tendency to spend and buy as a means to escape from conventionality. Quite a number of those surveyed had the feeling that more pioneering products and services were available than in the previous year.

Innovative ideas and new products with original design are in demand. Sometimes functionality is allowed to fall victim to the fascination with design. The main thing is that the idea or the product is liked and is perceived as something that will make life easier or provide personal enrichment. This applies to the consumer's living environment and to the consumer's car.

According a report in *Nikkei Weekly* (2004a), the Japanese car manufacturer Nissan found out that apparently higher-class interior fittings go down well in a vehicle model aimed specifically at the baby boomer generation. Nissan therefore fitted the model with better-quality textiles and well-designed seats as feel and appearance play a major role in the final decision to buy than does the price.

With differentiation of quality and value over price, much rides on the design, through which it is possible to reinforce the emotional attachment to a product or a service. In Japan, customer-related product design and presentation is playing an increasing role in objects that can be acquired everywhere.

Targeting specific groups

As well as products that attract a wide spectrum of buyers, the number of highly specialized products aimed at a small segment of buyers is increasing. Accordingly, target group–specific and individualized marketing in Japan has grown in importance compared to mass marketing. Customers readily accept a higher price for products which are manufactured and offered in spite of only a limited potential for sales, as long as a recognizable compromise is reached between price and value, and their chosen lifestyle is enhanced.

Suppliers of brand products are directing their marketing strategy at winning loyal customers and competitive advantage more strongly with flagship shops along the most important shopping streets in Japan. With costly shop fittings, a calm atmosphere with an uninterrupted supply of new activities and products, they attempt to win the emotional attachment of Japanese consumers who are becoming increasingly selective.

Women are heavily targeted, as they have plenty of buying power and are enthusiastic consumers. In order to offer a varied and attractive range of products to suit the lifestyle aspirations of Japanese women, individual companies are forced to design products and services for certain groups of women. According to *Nikkei Weekly* (2004b), individual companies have formed their dedicated all-women teams who look at the development of new products and services from a female point of view.

Furthermore, companies are relying more on younger buyers who spend less per purchase but who return frequently provide effective advertising and initiate more purchases. This applies both to high-quality clothing and cosmetics and to electronic devices.

Electrical and electronic products have advanced to become lifestyle products. For example, flat-screen televisions have developed into a highly popular purchase not only because they offer new audio-visual options but also because they lend new flair for interior design and furthermore are space-saving. DVD recorders also belong to the group of products which increase personal freedom.

Nowadays, intelligent recording devices can store the owner's personal viewing habits and search for suitable programmes from the range available. They record them during transmission by the recorder and they are then available for the consumer to play without the need to make complicated settings in advance. The individual still has the choice of keeping or deleting the recorded material.

Lifestyle influences

Lifestyle is very strongly driven by information and communication. Magazines, newspapers and advertising plus talking to friends and acquaintances are very important as sources of information on topics, items and services which improve the quality of life. Furthermore, in recent years, the Internet – via computer or mobile telephone – has become another option with which to find out about the latest trends.

It might be surprising to hear that in a survey of Internet users in Japan who were asked how using it influenced their lifestyles, the answers tended to indicate that it resulted in more contact with friends and family. On the other hand, the time for shopping, reading books or newspapers and leisure time in general fell, according to a study by the Ministry of Public Management, Home Affairs, Posts and Telecommunications (2004).

Companies will have to focus more on adjusting to the changes that result from demographic developments and influence lifestyle. The number of pensioner households will rise and at the same time the average size of household will fall. In particular, the proportion of single-person households and childless households will grow, according to trends identified on the basis of the National Institute of Population and Social Security Research (2000).

The two latter groups have in common that they spend more on consumer goods per head and spend their income and savings increasingly on higher value productions and services, such as cars and home furnishings, that will do justice to their lifestyle aspirations. It can also be assumed that the current generation of pensioners have high pension bonuses and savings, some of which they are consuming themselves and some of which they will pass down to their heirs, which provides them in turn with more buying power.

Lifestyle without limits

Although Japan is no longer the only trendsetter in Asia, it continues to be an ideal test market for lifestyle products and services. If a product sells well to Japan's very demanding consumers, then there is a high probability that it will market successfully in other markets in the region.

Japan in the grip of the organic wave – A new trend

The proportion of ecological products to total goods produced and total food supplied is still very small. However, high potential for growth is expected, as an increasing number of consumers now set great store by healthy, safe food. The LOHAS ("Lifestyle of Health and Sustainability") consumer groups with their preference for healthy and environmentally friendly products have many supporters.

According to a study by E-Square Inc. 29 per cent of the adult population fall into the LOHAS category. There is an even distribution of males and females and the weighting within age groups is also relatively uniform, with a slightly higher proportion of over-60s. LOHAS consumers are particularly receptive to organically grown products, nutritional supplements and natural cosmetics. In 2006, this group of consumers was the target of the "BioFach" trade fair, part of a larger exhibition which combined organically grown food, natural products and health care products under the concept of "Health Life Japan". BioFach took place from 21 to 23 September at the trade fair centre Tokyo Big Sight. Because demand from the LOHAS consumer segment, which mainly consists of high earners, is rising, the number of restaurants basing their menus on organic products is increasing. Supermarkets are also indicating a lot of interest in including more organic foods on their shelves. However, this demand cannot be fully met, because supplies of these products fall short.

Domestic production in particular is low, even though the Watami Food Group, for example, is expanding its network of organic farms every year. The opportunities to service a variety of distribution paths are currently still limited. The consumers are currently still members in one of the distribution organizations for organic products or have direct contact with the suppliers, either through direct sales or through Internet orders from local producers.

Due to the limited production, imports of fresh agricultural products from organic farms and of processed products are rising. The total amount of imported organic foods is exceeding the domestic production by some way and is likely to increase in the future. This means that for international companies in the food and agricultural sector there are considerable market opportunities in this new and growing market in Japan.

5.6   *Keiretsu* structures and intensity of competition

Keiretsu structures developed and consolidated over decades have shown signs of breaking down over recent years, which means that for many of the foreign companies doing business in Japan today the traditional *keiretsu* ties that still exist no longer represent a significant problem (Bosse 2000; Rossmann 2005). However, despite partial opening up of the *keiretsu* system, these powerful corporate networks have not yet completely disappeared from the market and in isolated cases can make Japanese business more difficult for foreign participants in the market.

Competition is highly intense in many Japanese markets and the large number of competing companies aggravate the situation further. Many of the competitors are, however, relatively small and play a part only on a national level. From the point of view of foreign market participants, Japanese companies compete primarily with

- price and
- personal networks that have developed over many years.

Foreign companies have the option of using differentiation strategies to avoid the strong competition on prices in many of the price-intensive markets. Japanese consumers have a great deal of buying power which offers a lot of room for creative product differentiation with clever combinations of quality, image and price. Furthermore, an intensively competitive, highly innovative environment (for example, in marketing or technology) can also initiate learning processes in a company.

The high prices in Japan, which represent a considerable advantage where they can be achieved (products in the upper price and performance brackets), reveal their negative side when operating costs are taken into account. Japan is still an expensive location, even though the prices for rents and staff are stagnating or falling slightly. The only compensation is that the boom prices of the 1980s are now consigned to the annals of Japanese economic history.

In order to continue to lead in price and quality, global Japanese companies are investing in their competitive power. The profits earned over the last few years have largely been channelled into

- new product development
- advanced product processes and
- research and development.

In the area of Human Resources, many companies are trying to reorganize the traditional Japanese working principles to reduce costs and increase margins (also see the World of Work, p. 124):

- The principle of lifelong employment has been watered down with part-time work, temporary employment and by moving jobs for which fewer qualifications are required out of the country (Haak 2001c).
- The seniority principle (promotion dependent on age and company) is giving way increasingly to more critical internal competition.
- Company unions are becoming increasingly significant with the more aggressive competition and go hand in hand with employees' corporate awareness.

5.7   Barriers to trade and pre-defined distribution systems

In the 1970s and 1980s, one of the key problems with entering and penetrating the market in Japan was posed by customs duty. Today, this is hardly significant; however, non-tariff barriers can occasionally cause difficulties for companies entering the still differentiated Japanese markets. Although many local standards have been brought into line with international standards there is still a need to modernize aging structures. Adapting local standards to developments in international technology frequently means a time-consuming legislative change which must be put through by the Japanese government.

For decades, the Japanese distribution system was characterized by many layers of dealers. However, the years of recession have strengthened Japanese dealers in their efforts to question traditional business relationships and to abandon them in favour of better suppliers in order to improve profits by reducing costs with new purchasing and sales arrangements.

Since the early 1990s, the number of intermediate dealers in the Japanese distribution systems has fallen and direct supply which bypasses these dealers is on the increase. This allows foreign companies more opportunities for penetrating the market by building up their own sales and service networks.

Furthermore, e-business is booming in Japan. In 2003, e-business expanded by more than two-thirds (Table 5.2). Creating virtual market places has also made Japanese trade and distribution systems

Table 5.2 Japanese e-business: Market volume (in billions of JPY by fiscal year)

Product/service 2003	Market volume	Share in percent of total industry sales
Automotive	28 049	57.8
Electronic, information and communication equipment	24 294	45.3
Information and software services	2 009	20.1
Steel, other metals, raw materials	5 367	13.5
Insurance services	3 934	12.0
Industrial machines, precision instruments	3 736	7.5
Textiles, consumer goods	2 066	6.2
Construction	3 549	4.1
Paper, office supplies	490	2.8
Transport, travel services	767	3.0
Chemicals	1 430	2.5
Food	1 403	2.4
Other	325	0.3
Total	77 432	11.2

Source: Maurer (2004a, p. 8).

more efficient in recent years. However, the potential for e-business has not yet been completely exhausted. Particularly, small and medium-sized businesses are not yet using the option of electronic procurement to a large extent (Maurer 2004a).

5.8 Industries of the future

Japan continues to maintain and expand those industries intensive in capital and know-how. Particularly, the sectors that dominate the Japanese economy namely

- chemicals
- mechanical engineering
- electronics and
- automotive

have had a strong presence in recent years. Four other sectors are currently the focus of interest for the Japanese government and for companies, with favourable growth prospects and the promise of taking over or securing market leadership for the Japanese economy in the future. They are biotechnology with annual growth rate of around 15 per cent; nanotechnology for improving products and opening up new areas of business; information and communications technology, and development of new generations of mobile communication aids and robotics. Japan leads the world in the production and application of industrial robots, and are hoping that the development of "intelligent", humanoid robots (for example, Asimo developed by Honda) will provide a strongly growing market in the future.

The Japanese government also has high hopes that the development of industry clusters will revitalize the economy with innovative products and processes. It intends to promote sharing and networking amongst scientific, industrial and state institutions to stimulate new research and development, with the ultimate aim of creating new innovative businesses. For example, in the area of biotechnology, the beginning of 2004 saw the creation of 14 large industrial areas extending from the south of Japan (Fukuoka Bio Valley Project) via Kobe (Medical Industry Development Project) to the north (Hokkaido

Bio Cluster). Were foreign companies to join these Japanese industrial and scientific networks, it could pay off in a long-term improvement in their competitive position in Japan.

The most important biotechnology clusters in Japan include the following:

- Hokkaido Bio Cluster
- Chiba Bio Life Science Network Forum
- Metropolitan Biotechnology -related Start-ups Network
- Yokohama Science Frontier
- Bio Factory Central Japan
- Fuji Pharm Valley Project
- Kansei Science Centre
- Kinki Bio-related Industry Project
- Hiroshima Central Bio-cluster
- Kagawa Rare Sugar Cluster
- Fukuoka Bio-Valley Project
- Kobe Medical Industry Development Project
- Saito Life Science Park and
- Toyama Pharmaceutical Bio-cluster.

Industry clusters have also developed in the field of nanotechnology in recent years (Table 5.3). Among the six most important nanotechnology industry clusters the "Intellectual Clusters" play a special role: currently there are 11 "Intellectual Clusters" throughout Japan where new research and development work is carried out in the field of

Table 5.3 Nanotechnology clusters in Japan

Prefecture	Research fields
Nagano	Smart device Carbon nanofibres & nanotubes
Aichi	Nanotechnology & nanomaterials research cluster
Kyoto	Nanotechnology cluster; nano-bio; nano-apparatus; nanoprocessing
Kita-Kyushu	Kita-Kyushu human technology cluster
Toyama	Medical biotechnology cluster (Toyama Medical-Bio Cluster)
Tokushima	Medical technology

Source: Maurer (2004b, p. 13).

nanotechnology. Government support for the development of industry and intellectual clusters through METI and MEXT (Ministry of Education, Culture, Sports, Science and Technology) is seeking to strengthen horizontal, and therefore multi-sector, networks (Maurer 2004b).

5.9   Positive overall picture

Closer analysis reveals the difficulties and imponderabilities of the Japanese market often cited by both foreign and Japanese business people to be conditions which, with the right knowledge and experience, turn out to be easily overcome. Following are some factors which strengthen the positive overall image of conducting business successfully in Japan.

- healthy economic growth;
- development of new and future-proof branches of industry and science;
- deregulation of Japanese policies;
- increased market transparency and
- the relaxation of the rigid structures forming the traditional Japanese company networks, particularly the supplier and distribution systems.

Eventually, the positive effects of overcoming the economic crisis will also be felt; the economic difficulties suffered by many Japanese companies in previous years have led to the dissolution of the inherited structures and systems which were detrimental to the prospects of foreign companies on the Japanese market.

6
Market Entry and Market Development Strategies – Opportunities for Foreign Companies in Japan

There are numerous ways to achieve success in the Japanese market and to maintain a leading position in the long term. The most familiar ways of entering and penetrating the market include the following:

- licensing;
- direct or indirect export;
- establishing an independent sales office;
- setting up franchising system;
- founding a joint venture;
- entering into a strategic alliance;
- founding a subsidiary of one's own company; or
- acquiring a Japanese company (Kutschker and Schmid 2002).

The reality of business in Japan is so extremely complex that theory-driven strategies for prospecting international markets in textbook format would be of no help to international managers. Other managers' theories and experience can convey key information on strategic planning and on how to use market entry and market development tools, but they cannot replace personal experience acquired from doing business on a day-to-day basis, from communicating with partner companies and from dealing with competitors and market players in Japan.

International managers must ask themselves this key question: which strategies for moving into and developing the market in Japan should I choose today to allow me to compete successfully tomorrow and make good profits the day after tomorrow? Using personal experience and researching at the right institutions (see below), a manager doing business in Japan can draw up an interpretation grid for evaluating alternative ways of proceeding as an aid to decision-making against the background of his theoretical knowledge.

6.1   Initial preparations for entering the market

The large body of literature in economics and management teaching contains repeated attempts to identify theoretical models or conceptual reference frameworks for selecting the correct strategy for market entry and development. Management-oriented institutions doing research on Japan, business consultants and application-oriented economic institutions have come up with numerous empirical studies which explicitly try to explain which factors play a role in the choice of a market entry and development strategy and how they are weighted.

In view of the sometimes contradictory results of empirical studies and theoretical approaches, precise information on which strategy to select in each instance for entering and developing the Japanese market is not very promising (Anderson 1997). There are numerous factors influencing the choice which management must examine for relevance to each instance of market entry and market development in Japan. The advantages and disadvantages of the possible alternatives must be evaluated against the background of the individual company profile with its strong and weak points. In the analysis of external factors such as

- the economic development of the country,
- current economic policy
- and sector specific conditions in Japan

management can make use of documentation, analyses and evaluations from the relevant scientific, private, policy-formulating or practice-oriented institutions. These are, for example in a German case:

- the German Chamber of Industry and Trade in Japan (DIHKJ);
- the German Embassy in Tokyo;
- JETRO;
- the Deutsch–Japanischer Wirtschaftskreis (DJW) (an organization offering support for German businesses in Japan);
- business consultancies;
- universities;
- research institutions, such as the German Institute for Japanese Studies (DIJ);
- associations and so on.

One of the oldest ways of establishing contacts and acquiring business is to attend trade fairs. Trade fairs in Japan are obvious venues where contact can be made with Japanese business partners, but this is also possible at other international trade fairs (Table 6.1). First impressions of business partners, markets, technological development, and the opportunities and risks associated with prospecting a market can be formed at trade fairs. Approximately 1000 trade fairs take place in Japan every year and of these approximately 400 have international relevance. The semiconductor trade fair "Semicon", the Tokyo Motor Show and "Ambiente", the trade fair for consumer goods, are among the most attractive in Japan for German businesses.

Table 6.1 Main trade fair locations in Japan

Location	Exhibition area
Kanazawa	22 453 m^2
Kobe International Exhibition Hall	18 760 m^2
West Japan General Exhibition Hall (Kita-Kyushu)	20 757 m^2
Marine trade fair Fukuoka	40 315 m^2
Kyoto International Exhibition Hall	27 772 m^2
INTEX Osaka	114 054 m^2
Axes Sapporo	42 463 m^2
Tokyo Big Sight	192 127 m^2
Makuhari trade fair Chiba	75 751 m^2
Pacifico Yokohama	31 444 m^2
Port trade fair Nagoya	68 284 m^2

Source: *Japanmarkt*, December 2004, p. 7.

Selecting the relevant trade fairs

The Federal Ministry for Economy (Bundeswirtschaftsministerium) offers an orientation programme for selecting appropriate trade fairs which it supports jointly with the Association of the German Trade Fair Industry (AUMA). To find, choose and organize trade fairs and conferences help should be sought from JETRO for the specific product or services offered by the foreign company. The German Office for Foreign Trade (bfai) and the DIHKJ also have information on trade fairs in Japan.

Japanese business people as a rule see trade fairs only as places in which to establish contact, gather information, examine products and carry out reconnaissance, or possibly to consolidate previously made contacts, and not as a place to acquire business or conclude contracts in haste.

The most important trade fairs with a clear international orientation are to be found in the two main economic regions.

- Kanto (Tokyo, Chiba, Kawasaki and Yokohama) and
- Kansai (Osaka, Kobe and Kyoto).

biggest trade fair locations are

- Tokyo Big Sight – the most important trade fair location in Japan,
- INTEX Osaka and
- Makuhari trade fair in Chiba.

6.2 Licensing

There is a very simple strategy for entering and developing in the Japanese market: licensing, which applies mainly to the areas of research and development and production and sales. The following aspects must be considered here:

- patents
- utility models
- registered designs
- trademarks (brands)
- copyright

- technical know-how and
- commercial know-how.

The advantages of licensing are obvious: licenses allow the licensor to market assets that are already successful at home (for example, patents or brands), parallel in Japan without a great deal of effort, thus generating additional income (Macharzina and Oesterle 2002). The income received in the country of the licensee shortens the pay-back period for investments. Assets that have arrived at the end of their life in the foreign company's country can continue to generate value when licensed to a Japanese partner. Licensing avoids trans-port costs, minimizes risks with exchange rates, and entry into the Japanese market can be faster than if a company sets up its own branch office, for example.

Another crucial advantage of licensing is that it consumes few resources. The costs are incurred primarily in selecting the right licensee in Japan, in drawing up a suitable licensing agreement and – the effort involved here should not be underestimated – in monitoring adherence to the licensing agreement.

Character figures from cartoons, comics or video games are very popular objects in the licensing business, but there are other products which find a market in Japan. Licensing agencies assist in contact-ing manufacturers, distributors and retailers. Japanese licensees are frequently knowledgeable about the local market, which often goes hand in hand with a well-developed customer base and the tradi-tional personal relationships with business people – precisely those factors which make it considerably easier to start doing business in Japan. However, for deeper penetration of the market with a more long-term perspective, licensing on its own is not sufficient.

Knowing how the Japanese market and Japanese companies in the same sector develop in terms of their technology and business practice ensures definite competitive advantage. Licensing as a sole market development strategy does not facilitate the accumulation of expertise specific to Japan. What does the competition in the Japanese and in the other Asian markets do to achieve competitive advantage and take the lead in strategic business areas? Only those businesses directly involved in Japan can find out.

Another problem with licensing is the danger of building up a strong Japanese competitor for the future which will put the know-how gained through the licensing business to its own use. For this reason, patents, utility models, registered designs and trademarks should be registered in Japan early on. This goes hand in hand with the fundamental difficulty of finding a trustworthy Japanese partner who will contribute the achievement potential and the economic and technical requirements for entering into a licensing agreement. Selecting an unsuitable partner can lead to

- production quality problems
- a lack of commitment in marketing or
- even image problems with the target group in Japan.

The licensing agreement should define precisely the object of the license and the licensed territory. Legal advice obtained on site in Japan is essential for drawing up the detail of the agreement. Advice should be sought from the Chamber for Foreign Trade in Tokyo and the relevant consultancies in Japan in advance, as these institutions have specific knowledge and experience of licensing.

It makes undeniable sense to use licensing as a way to profit from the Japanese market without making a large financial commitment. However, the licensor must be clear that many Japanese markets change more quickly and dynamically than similar markets in other countries. In concrete terms, this means that the Japanese licensee can in a few years be in a position to develop and make available for the Japanese market technology superior to that existing at the time when the license was issued.

For years now there has been another noticeable tendency threatening foreign market participants with a danger that is not to be underestimated: Japanese businesses develop products with a foreign image in order to establish themselves in Japan as a brand with international ranking. This deprives the foreign licensor of considerable competitive advantage, that of having a foreign image, right from the start.

Before any decisions are made, companies should investigate whether issuing a license to a Japanese company will not, in the end, deny them successful access to the Japanese market and prevent them from developing the market in the long term and whether it would create a possible competitor whose competition could extend to other markets.

6.3 Low risk: Indirect exports

Indirect exports require the help of a third party. Foreign trade with Japan is carried out via agents inland. The relationship between the exporter and the Japanese business partner is maintained indirectly via an intermediary in the country of the exporter. Indirect export to Japan via export agents or trading houses is relatively low risk for the inland company, as it supplies Japan via an inland foreign trade company or an inland export house. The company is not itself taking the risk of going into Japan, but acting through an intermediary in its own country (Bellmann and Haak 2005).

Distributors can be export agents or trading houses who buy products at home and take on all the work and costs of exporting them. They act at their own risk and also take the risk of selling, unlike export agents who export at the manufacturer's risk – leaving the major risks and costs with the producer.

Where knowledge of the Japanese market is scant, this simple form of market prospecting is ideal for gathering information for use in the future and for gaining closer experience of Japanese business practices. Later on, the company can move to a higher level of market prospecting and market development.

The advantages of indirect export via trading houses and export agents require no further explanation:

- protection for the financial and personnel resources of the manufacturer at home;
- export risks are borne by distributors in Japan; and
- exploitation of the distributor's specific market knowledge in Japan.

Rapid expansion into Japan is made easier by distributors as they can use existing customer relationships. They also contribute experience in dealing with customs formalities and official permits (Kutschker and Schmid 2002).

The disadvantages of this form of prospecting the market are also obvious:

- some of the profit stays with the distributor;
- the distributor's position in the market and knowledge places the foreign manufacturer in a dependent position;

- the foreign manufacturer does not have direct contact with the customers in the Japanese markets.

The foreign manufacturer relies heavily on the commitment of the export agent. If the agent represents several suppliers then it can easily happen that one of them is neglected. Furthermore, the manufacturer has only a limited influence on the way marketing policy is implemented.

6.4   Direct export

Exporting directly to Japan can avoid some of the negative effects of indirect export as there are no inland intermediaries in the foreign trade, allowing a direct relationship between a non-Japanese and a Japanese business partner.

This means that the exporting company is able to exercise some control over the business in Japan. The direct nature of the export process also allows complex products or services which would not be suitable for sales via a foreign trade company or export house to be exported. Although there is more effort involved in direct export to Japan than in indirect export, the costs can still be described as relatively low, compared to other forms of market entry and development, such as establishing a sales office in Japan. Nevertheless, investment is required to develop a more complex relationship with customers and business partners.

One advantage of exporting directly to Japan which should not be underestimated is that the exporting company gains specific knowledge of Japan, which can provide a good basis for selecting subsequent strategies for market entry and development. Switching to an alternative form of market penetration is easier starting from direct export than from most other options.

To establish a more complex relationship Japan offers a choice between the foreign trading houses, the internationally active Japanese Universal Trading Houses (*sogo shosha*) and also the specialized Japanese import companies. The exporter hands over the import business and the distribution to the agent. An exclusive agreement should be drawn up to allow the exporter to continue to have some influence on marketing policy (sales prices, sales campaigns, product presentation and so on). It should specify clearly defined and monitored minimum expenses for target-oriented marketing (Bellmann and Haak 2005).

Companies considering direct export should establish whether the agent they select can actually give the products the attention they need in Japan. Skilled sales engineers and a superbly well-trained service staff are essential for selling technically complicated products that require a lot of explanation. Sales and advertising materials, technical explanations and comprehensive manuals on operating and maintaining the exported products must, of course, be available in Japanese.

To avoid distributors, there is the option of supplying a Japanese bulk buyer directly. However, this assumes

- good integration in the Japanese business environment;
- knowledge of the sales and distribution structures; and
- experience in dealing with Japanese authorities and competitors.

Supplying directly is often the cheapest way of penetrating the market in Japan. If the foreign company deploys its own representatives in Japan, the costs rise accordingly, but the advantages still predominate. The exporting company can observe the market directly through the representatives and acquire profound knowledge about Japanese consumers, their wishes and requirements and valuable information about the competitive environment in the Japanese markets.

As an alternative to going in alone, companies can enter into cooperative ventures with Japanese companies. For example, a cooperative sales and distribution venture with a Japanese company which manufactures and sells similar products might be considered (Haak, R. 2000).

The Japanese partner makes its sales and distribution network available and designs the marketing-mix tools, whilst the foreign partner broadens the Japanese company's range of services and its competence profile. However, the danger that the Japanese partner will copy the products cannot be excluded.

6.5 Franchising

Creating a franchise is primarily an issue of sales and distribution. In many cases, the foreign company hands over a long-established and tested management, sales and marketing concept to the Japanese franchisee.

The overall corporate concept becomes the object of a joint venture in the Japanese market between the foreign and the Japanese partners. In this case, a complete system is transferred to the Japanese instead of individual assets. The best-known examples in the Japanese market include

- McDonald's
- The Body Shop
- Pizza Hut and
- Kentucky Fried Chicken.

Franchising with a Japanese partner has numerous benefits for a foreign franchiser. The high-cost Japanese market can be penetrated without capital investment and the high buying power of Japanese consumers fully exploited. The capital for penetrating the market in Japan is provided mainly by the Japanese franchisee who must deal with the high staffing, rent and service costs. The risk of failing on the Japanese market is considerably minimized for the foreign company. If the franchiser's idea is well received in Japan, market development can be rapid, as demonstrated in impressive style by McDonald's.

The success of the whole franchising venture depends on the performance of the individual Japanese partners. Problems with one of the Japanese companies (for example, quality problems) can damage the reputation and image of the whole franchise in Japan. Although the franchiser has wide-ranging guidance and monitoring rights over the franchisee, there are fewer opportunities to exert influence than with a fully controlled subsidiary. Management of the franchise network in Japan is also extremely complicated and costly.

6.6   The sales office

Opening their own sales office is another way in which foreign companies can achieve a presence on the Japanese market. As the costs for staffing and rents are very high in Japan, this form of market entry and development needs to be justified by a sufficiently large sales volume and appropriate profit margins.

Points in favour of this alternative are that the company builds up an independent customer service department, which is very highly valued in Japan, and can gather information on market activity and on the competition directly. A good customer service department and a well-developed service network are essential for complex and technically sophisticated products in many Japanese markets.

There is frequently another problem besides the high costs: recruiting suitable Japanese personnel, particularly engineers, who not only have technical expertise but also language skills and who are prepared to work for a long term for a foreign company in Japan.

The Japanese labour market has become more mobile over recent years. Nevertheless, the search for exceptional Japanese staff demands the investment of considerable resources. Many Japanese employees still expect lifelong employment in a highly regarded company. However, concessions in this respect should not be made when Japanese staff are appointed, unless lifelong employment fits in with the personnel management's usual practice.

It is advisable to look around not just in Japan, but also abroad (for example, London, Dusseldorf or New York) for future employees. Japanese business partners, who frequently have well-developed personal networks, can also be called upon to help look for high-quality staff. Advertising in the newspapers is not on its own a suitable approach.

6.7   Setting up a joint venture

The problems described above, of finding highly qualified Japanese personnel for the business, often prompt companies to consider establishing a joint venture. The staff required for market development are supplied by the Japanese partner in this case. However, it is not advisable to set up a joint venture merely because of the need to find suitable personnel (Zentes, Swoboda and Morschett 2003).

Joint ventures allow rapid access to the Japanese market and are chosen in many cases for this reason. Compared to developing a joint venture, establishing a new subsidiary takes a very long time and also consumes a great deal of resources, which are then not available for market prospecting strategies.

One reason for entering into a joint venture in Japan is the opportunity to use the local partner's knowledge to enter the highly competitive Japanese markets. Having a Japanese partner facilitates the organization of procurement and marketing, and makes contact with government bodies and bureaucracy much easier. A joint venture can thus combine complementary resources, skills and competences.

A joint venture can be sustainable in the long term only if the interests of the partners really complement each other. Both partners must be convinced that the shared company is essential to achieve success in the Japanese market (Perlitz and Seger 2000).

Partners wanting to enter into a joint venture should know each other well. The decision to establish the venture must result from a business relationship of many years standing. One of the most important prerequisites for successful management of a joint venture is a fully developed relationship based on trust. The partners in a joint venture are dependent on each other. They must consult each other about decisions and actions. With the geographical distance that separates the two countries of origin, coordination frequently takes a great deal of effort. It should also not be forgotten that profits are divided in a joint venture.

If the aims of the partners develop in different directions over time and their interests begin to diverge, the continued existence of the joint venture could be in danger. Joint ventures, like other cooperative forms of foreign market development, can lead to a leaking of expertise. This outflow of technical knowledge can seriously threaten the existence of the joint venture if the flow of know-how originally agreed implicitly or explicitly between the partners is unilaterally exceeded, causing the gains in learning and knowledge to be concentrated primarily with one joint venture partner.

The success of a joint venture also depends on the goals of the partners, which can be very different. In this respect it is difficult to give general advice on successful management in a joint venture. Empirical studies repeatedly cite the following factors in successful corporate collaborations:

- know and evaluate the strengths and weaknesses of your own company;
- know and evaluate the strengths and weaknesses of your partner's company;
- think in terms of benefits for both sides to create win-win situations;

- learn from conflict;
- encourage communication within and between the companies;
- seek consensus;
- encourage staff development;
- demonstrate flexibility and
- provide motivated and high-performing staff for the management of the joint venture (Steinmann and Schreyögg 1997).

As a joint venture is a company with two or more partners in Japan, that is a "new" company with its own legal personality, the contract must contain provisions for amicable agreement should the interests of the partners involved diverge.

In practical terms, it is perfectly possible for the collaboration to affect only some areas of the company (for example, only production or certain areas in research and development). The joint venture can also encompass several areas or include the complete value-added chain with all the activities involved.

The time frame of a joint venture in Japan can vary; it can be limited or set up for the long term. A time-limited arrangement is appropriate for both sides if the motives for engaging in the joint venture will no longer apply for both partners after a certain period. This scenario is very likely to arise in a research and development project. In practice, however, contracts for most joint ventures in Japan are drawn up without a time limit, which is illustrated by the large number of long-term joint ventures that have operated successfully in Japan.

Frequently, mistakes are made when the Japanese and foreign companies start to negotiate the establishment of a joint venture, as their different views regarding the planned objectives and the deployment of resources are seldom differentiated in discussion. Subjects such as

- the images of the foreign and the Japanese companies;
- the new image of the joint venture;
- the form taken by the personnel policy;
- the payment and number of expatriates;
- the degree to which the marketing mix is adapted;
- the resolution of conflict;
- the use of technological innovation

are some of the key aspects which should be discussed in detail during negotiations to establish a joint venture in Japan and which should be included in the agreement.

For example, the decision to appoint new staff as soon as possible for the joint venture instead of just taking on employees from the Japanese partner should be set down early on. Independent recruitment will in the long term encourage company loyalty to the joint venture. Employees delegated by the Japanese parent company should be offered the option after some time of continuing to work in the joint venture or of taking a higher-level job with the Japanese parent. Allowing a decision to be taken maintains motivation, as the possibility of promotion in the parent company is still available after a spell in the joint venture.

6.8   Building up strategic alliances

Another form of cooperative market entry and market development strategy is the strategic alliance which in most cases is not confined to a national market, but which extends beyond country borders. An example of a successful strategic alliance between a Japanese company and several international participants is that entered into by the Japanese airline All Nippon Airways (ANA). This is the Star Alliance, in which it cooperates with the airlines Lufthansa, Thai Airways, Austrian Airlines, Air Canada, United Airlines, SAS, Singapore Airlines, VARIG, Air New Zealand, Mexicana Airlines, British Midland and Ansett Australia.

A characteristic of the strategic alliance is that the foreign companies and the Japanese partner(s) agree to cooperate in a precisely defined area that has strategic relevance for both (or all) of them. The collaboration is not intended to realize a short-term and time-limited objective, such as is frequently the case with simple cooperative projects, but is a long-term plan to strengthen the strategic competitiveness of the corporate partners.

Unlike in a joint venture, a joint company is not established in Japan, which means that there is no capital investment on either side. The benefits and motives and the problems and disadvantages of strategic alliances bear great similarity to those of the joint venture.

A central motive is to achieve scale effects which could not be realized by the partners separately. This form of cooperation between foreign and one or more Japanese companies allows strategic alliances to gain access to complementary resources, skills and competences which the participating companies could not have achieved on their own. Also,

- sharing the business risk
- and rapid entry into the Japanese market

are amongst the main motives for forming a strategic alliance with Japanese companies. The concurrence of several motives for entering into a strategic alliance is demonstrated by numerous empirical studies (Kutschker and Schmid 2002).

The problems and disadvantages are also well documented in the relevant scientific and practical journals. For example, like other forms of market entry and development, strategic alliances have to comply with the requirements of Japanese competition law. There is a fundamental risk that the legal situation in Japan will not allow the intentions of the alliance partners to be realized.

The requirement for coordination and agreement is extremely high in strategic alliances and in the long term, involuntary loss of know-how to the partners can also become a problem. To be successful with a strategic alliance first and foremost requires an exceptional personnel policy, as entering into, developing and nurturing a strategic alliance all require different managers to be qualified in different ways. Trust and commitment are the two key factors which determine whether the collaboration between Japanese and foreign companies will succeed on a strategic level.

6.9 The subsidiary

What are the motives for setting up a one hundred per cent subsidiary – the most costly form of market entry and development strategy in Japan? Image alone is a very significant reason for maintaining a subsidiary in Japan. A key advantage over other market entry and market development strategies, which are frequently integrated in cooperative ventures to achieve their goals, is the high level of independence, the fact that the company does not have to rely on a third party (for example, a licensee or a joint venture partner).

Having sole responsibility makes it easier to impose company strategies as there is no need for lengthy and costly consultation processes. Competitive advantage achieved by the company remains its own; there is no danger of involuntary knowledge transfer (Macharzina and Osterle 2002).

Setting up a subsidiary is one of the most difficult tasks in a market entry and development strategy in Japan. The basic problem is staffing the new establishment with qualified Japanese employees who can contribute both business contacts and sufficient knowledge of the market and of the competition to make the start-up successful. It can take a very long time to put together a good team of specialist personnel for the subsidiary as financial incentive is not one of the main motivations for a Japanese manager to move from a respected Japanese company to a foreign firm. The job change is often seen as an indication of personal difficulties and not as a sign of increased flexibility.

It is important that qualified Japanese are appointed to important positions in subsidiaries in order to overcome difficulties with the Japanese distribution system, nurture contacts with the authorities and business partners, and to build up an appropriate personal network.

A further issue that should not be underestimated is that in the early phases of establishing a subsidiary it is difficult to develop the necessary group thinking as the new employees come from different areas and have had different work and career experience. Frequently, employees are selected mainly based on their linguistic ability, but technical and managerial qualifications should play an equal part in personnel decisions.

Unlike in joint ventures or strategic alliances, the risks of doing business in Japan are not shared. Withdrawal from Japan is not so easy as with other forms of market entry and development, because in establishing the subsidiary the company has entered into a kind of declaration of obligation towards Japan. The subsidiary therefore bears considerable responsibility for the status of the company in the Japanese and the international markets. Bad management decisions made by underqualified employees are a significant danger in a subsidiary's start-up phase.

6.10   Mergers and acquisitions

Mergers and acquisitions are worth considering as an option for doing business in Japan. Since the second half of the 1990s, the chances of prospecting the Japanese market in this way have been very good because company valuations are very low. None of the time-consuming and costly procedures are associated with establishing a subsidiary and market development can proceed rapidly.

Legal obstacles are not an impediment to this way of entering the market. However, it is often not easy to find a suitable Japanese firm for sale. The situation has changed in favour of foreign business recently, but this form of market entry and development also has its problematic side. In almost all cases, both the takeover and the merger are successful alternatives for moving into and developing the market only if there are existing long-standing business connections and a position of great trust has been built up and nurtured. Even where these long-term business relationships are in place, careful preparation subjecting the market and the competition to thorough analysis is essential.

7
From Theory to Practice: The World of Business in Japan

7.1 Planning a business trip

Preparing for a business trip to Japan takes time. The following factors must be taken into account:

- finding suitable dates for the visit;
- deciding on the participants;
- letter of introduction from a person known to both companies;
- involving interpreters at an early stage;
- thank you letters when dates have been agreed;
- Japanese-standard business cards;
- attire; and
- gifts.

The Business year begins on 1 April and ends on 31 March. Timing a visit during the budget period, particularly in March and September (half-year accounts) is not ideal as Japanese managers are busy with planning and final accounts during this time.

The accumulation of public holidays at the end of April and the beginning of May is called "Golden Week". Many Japanese companies close for a whole week, making it the time when Japanese people are most likely to travel. It is vital to book flights, trains and hotels as early as possible. This is not a particularly suitable time for a business trip. It might also be difficult to agree business dates in mid-July and mid-August (*o-bon*) and at the end of the year (*o-shogatsu*) as these are the times of Japan's main family festivals.

Public holidays in Japan are listed below:

- 1 January (New Year, *ganjitsu*)
- 10 January (Coming-of-age Day, *seijinnohi*)
- 11 February (National Foundation Day, *kenkokukinenbi*)
- 21 March (Spring Equinox, *shunbunnohi*)
- 29 April (Greenery Day, *midorinohi*)
- 3 May (Constitution Day, *kempokinenbi*)
- 5 May (Children's Day, *kodomonohi*)
- 18 July (Ocean Day, *uminohi*)
- 19 September (Respect for the Aged Day, *keironohi*)
- 23 September (Autumnal Equinox, *shubunnohi*)
- 10 October (Sports Day, *taiikunohi*)
- 3 November (Culture Day, *bunkanohi*)
- 23 November (Labour Day, *kinrokanshanohi*)
- 23 December (Emperor's Birthday, *tennonotanjobi*)

When selecting the people who are to take part in the business trip to Japan, ensure that the delegation includes a senior manager; rank and status are very important to Japanese business people. A representative from an equivalent level of management on the Japanese side will take part in the discussions (Winkels and Schlütermann-Sugiyama 2000).

In Japan, a letter of introduction is the classic way to gain access to new customers or suppliers. It is also advisable when building up a new partnership between companies. The letter of introduction describes the benefits of a new business relationship and emphasizes the special features of the Japanese and European companies. The letter of introduction should be written by someone

- with whom both the European company and the company that is being contacted are closely associated;
- who enjoys a special social status; or
- to whom the future business partner feels obliged owing to a business relationship of many years.

The trusted third party is ideally familiar with the business customs in the Japanese company and can therefore provide information before the visit takes place and can contact the right people there, which represents a significant time-saving.

The significance of a letter of introduction not only for initiating but also for building on business relationships in Japan should not be underestimated. Nurturing personal relationships with Japanese business partners, which entails the development of a relationship based on much mutual trust, is a fundamental investment for building up competitive advantage in Japan. One of the main tasks undertaken by foreign managers in Japan and a condition for business success is the maintenance and development of personal networks to underpin the corporate relationships.

Interpreters should be employed to ensure that the business trip to Japan proceeds successfully, at least for the first visit. The interpreter should be selected not only on the basis of his/her faultless command of the technicalities of interpreting, but also for his/her familiarity with the Japanese mentality and with business customs in Japan and Europe. It would be a great advantage, particularly for the initial approaches, if he/she also knows about the products, technology and management principles of the company. For this reason it makes sense to take an interpreter from Europe along on the trip and involve him/her in the preparations (for example, preparing company documentation in Japanese) (Winkels and Schlütermann-Sugiyama 2000).

It can be a definite advantage if the interpreter not only attends the official business meetings, but also participates in the social activities (for example, restaurant visits, games of golf, excursions and so on). Much business and personal information that is not discussed in official surroundings is more likely to be shared in an informal setting.

The letter thanking the Japanese company for agreeing to the business meeting in Japan should contain the names, functions and positions of the people who will be setting off to Japan.

It is a clever idea to send the business cards of the participants in advance. Japanese managers appreciate being able to spend a lot of time preparing themselves thoroughly for pre-arranged meetings. On the other hand, they are not very keen on surprises: in unforeseeable situations they can appear extremely inflexible. However, if they get a precise picture of the visitors, their functions and their positions in the company from business cards, which they can pass on to different

gratitude; where mistakes have been made, [†]'
of apology. If foreign and Japanese business pa
ally, the gifts express liking. Gifts exchanged wh
parting for some time are an expression of gratitu
the relationship will continue. They are indispensab
of a child, at weddings and on bereavement. In Japan
special times of gift giving (New Year, summer) when gifts
stood as expressions of appreciation and respect, and hope
relationship will continue.

7.2 Duties in Japan

On the occasion of a first meeting, a table is frequently reserved for a subsequent meal. Although it is possible to turn down an invitation to a meal, pleading the long tiring journey, it would make a negative impression on the Japanese host; he could think that the representatives of the Western company are not interested in interpersonal relationships. The foundations for a long-term basis of trust between the companies should, according to Japanese custom, be laid with an informal meal in a pleasant atmosphere (Kobayashi 1996).

Eating in a restaurant is governed by special rituals. Generally, beer is drunk with the meal. The evening festivity starts as a rule with a toast, Japanese *kanpai*, in which the glasses raised should, if at all possible, still be full. Later the drink is frequently changed to sake; whisky and water are also popular. It is not considered wrong in Japan to be tipsy (not completely drunk) after working hours; on the contrary, it is part of having a good time together. Alcohol acts as a social lubricant, smoothing the way to establishing and maintaining social relationships.

As a rule, the host orders, after consulting briefly with all those present. If bottles are placed on the table, note that guests never fill their own glasses, but leave this to the host or the guests sitting next to them. They also top up glasses. Conversely, the guest should fill and top up the glasses of those sitting around him/her. This custom also applies in private homes.

The purpose of these evenings is to underpin the personal relationships. Certain liberties can be taken when the participants are tipsy. It is permitted to express amusement at Japanese characteristics, but foreign guests can also become the object of some curiosity. The question of whether or not they could really stomach all the delicacies of the Japanese cuisine and a childlike delight at identifying dishes that they would find inedible are particularly popular.

The Western guest is very much allowed to be infected by the general gaiety. However, he/she should never make the mistake of apologizing for his/her behaviour on the previous evening. This would result in an embarrassing atmosphere, as an apology of this nature would cast an unfavourable light on the Japanese host. The contrast between socially acceptable informality after hours and the seriousness of official negotiations are a routine part of business in Japan.

After the meal it is appropriate to issue a return invitation to Europe including a look round the European company. This skilfully combines thanks with gauging Japanese interest in a return invitation. If interest is expressed, then the Japanese managers are highly likely to want to enter into a business relationship with the European company.

Like most celebrations in Japan, a Japanese business meal lasts for around two hours. However, it is common for small groups to go to a nearby bar after the restaurant. A visit to one of the numerous karaoke bars is a popular amusement. The visitors are expected to join in the general fun of singing familiar pop songs in front of the audience. It is impossible for them to decline, unless they want earn for themselves the name of spoilsports with their future business partners right from the beginning of the discussions.

If the visitor takes on the role of host, there are some issues to note regarding payment. In Japan, it is considered extremely impolite and embarrassing if the bill is subjected to scrutiny in the restaurant, possibly even in front of the Japanese guests. The bill should be paid discreetly at the cash desk, as is usual in Japan. Tips are not given in restaurants in Japan, taxis or for any other services.

Business and private life are kept separate carefully in Japan. It is unusual and very much an exception for foreign business partners to be invited home by Japanese business people. If the Japanese partner reveals his private life, it creates a basis of trust which demands much commitment in response. The Japanese business partner expects similarly obliging and committed treatment on his return visit to Europe as a matter of course.

In Japan, people enter private apartments or houses – like shrines, temples, historical buildings, Japanese restaurants or changing rooms in some department stores – without shoes. Japanese hosts usually keep slippers for guests at the entrance. In the guest toilet there is another pair of slippers, which is used only in that room and must be left there itself. Rooms carpeted with *tatami* in restaurants, apartments and so on must be entered only with stockinged feet; slippers are not allowed.

How the discussion proceeds?

A first discussion with Japanese business partners starts by building up a good atmosphere for a meeting. Questions about how was the journey to Japan, how the hotel is and first impressions of the foreign country draw the guest into small talk which is important for the negotiations to come and to which he/she should submit patiently. There is no pressure at the first meeting to produce concrete results or even any decisions. It is not required to conduct weighty discussions and exchange different points of view and arguments, but to hold a conversation on a wide range of subjects to allow both sides to get to know each other.

A presentation of the company, the products and manufacturing processes and statements about its image and its position in the market are covered in the course of the conversation. Generally, all those things which previously were mentioned in the initial letter or which are already covered in the company website or in brochures are discussed. Information should be made available not only in the respective European language and English, but also in Japanese if at all possible.

Tip

Unwritten rule: Punctuality
Guests arriving too late for an appointment will fall considerably in the esteem of their opposite number. Appointments in Japan, particularly in the industrial centres, should be well spaced and enough time should be planned for long journeys and heavy traffic.

Late arrival at the first meeting would be interpreted as disinterest and fecklessness.

It could so happen that the Western delegation in Japan is outnumbered by the Japanese group and the first meeting proceeds hesitantly and with the exchange of few words. The visitors would be wrong to react with uncertainty and hectic hyperactivity. Instead, they should demonstrate a relaxed, calm attitude. These are characteristics that the Japanese interpret as signs of strength. As a rule, it is the Japanese managers who initiate the discussion and, after receiving positive signals, take it further. Patience is very important, because often the same questions are asked several times in different contexts during the discussion. With this repeated questioning, the Japanese managers collect confirmation of particularly interesting or critical aspects and check if the statements are consistent.

Tip

Seating arrangements
The seating arrangement adopted during the business meeting reveals information about the ranking of the managers in the Japanese company. The highest-ranking manager takes the most important place in the middle of the table. The lower ranks sit to his right and left in their hierarchical order. The guests are given places towards the rear of the room not with their backs to the door, but facing it. The discussion should not just concentrate around the highest-ranking participants, but involve all those present as far as possible, as later an employee taking part will be nominated as responsible for further contact.

In the first meeting, unsatisfactory proposals made by the Japanese side should not under any circumstances be rebuffed directly. Open criticism must always be avoided – this means not only criticism of the Japanese dialogue partners, but criticism of the visiting delegation amongst themselves. The atmosphere and the basic feeling of goodwill would suffer from the aggressive element of criticism. Important points of criticism should be discussed privately with the appropriate Japanese manager in a more informal atmosphere, a bar or a restaurant for example.

Honne and *tatemae* are the basic tenets on which Japanese behaviour is based to prevent critical, possibly embarrassing situations from even arising.

Tip

Honne and tatemae

The highest principle observed by the Japanese in their interaction with each other is *"honne* and *tatemae"*, which means roughly "true intention and façade" and is often circumscribed with "Japanese two-facedness". To maintain harmony between human beings (*wa*) it is considered very bad form, both privately and in business, to express an opinion directly and openly and not take into account the interests of the other participants (*honne*) even if what is said does not represent harsh criticism. Keeping quiet about and circumscribing (*tatemae*) true intentions is intended to avoid situations which the other side could interpret as confrontation.

7.3   Reaching decisions

An initial business meeting should not be expected to produce direct decisions and agreement from the Japanese side. As many Japanese companies apply the *ringi* system, a proposal or a plan passes through many different points in the company hierarchy. The more significant and extensive the issue, the more different Japanese office-holders and specialists are involved in the decision-making process. The time allocated to this process in a Japanese company is very generous.

Obstacle

No direct "no".

Japanese managers avoid the use of the direct "no", *iie* in Japanese. There are numerous flowery circumlocutions for "no". A typical example is the answer that there is no precedent set for something. Knowing that in Japan precedents are avoided as far as possible makes the repudiation obvious. Even formulations such as "I will look into the matter" or "I will speak to my senior managers about it" or even "I will do my best" would be interpreted as rejection on the part of the Japanese partner.

If an employee presents a proposal that goes beyond his/her competence, then he/she makes use of the *ringi* system. The employee makes an application to his senior managers describing the situation and the specific steps to take to implement it. If the proposal is evaluated positively by all the senior managers involved, then there are no obstacles to its implementation in the company. The action required is supported by all those involved as they have given their approval via the *ringi* system and share in the responsibility.

If the proposal is rejected on one of the higher levels, then it is returned to the employee responsible via the different levels in the hierarchy. He/she is requested to make changes and again pass the modified proposal to his immediate supervisors. As the proposal can be rejected at any level of the hierarchy and the employee is forced to take the suggestions for modification into account by revising the proposal, the process can take up large amounts of time. This explains the sometimes extremely long time it takes for a decision to be made in a Japanese company.

If the relationship with the Japanese company has existed for some years and the business partners already know each other through various business deals, the decision-making process can be accelerated with *nemawashi*. The *nemawashi* principle requires that a person of trust be identified in the Japanese company. This person should be familiar with the practical aspects of transacting business and also be in a position to make suggestions and also to hasten decisions (Kono and Clegg 2001).

Problematic subjects should be discussed before business meetings with this trusted representative from the Japanese side in the informal surroundings of a restaurant, a golf course or a bar. If you are successful in persuading this person for your cause, he will wield his influence positively so that, possibly, agreement can be reached before the official meeting without any unpleasant conflict (Winkels and Schlütermann-Sugiyama 2000).

The *nemawashi* and *ringi* systems often go hand in hand. It is not usual in Japan for decisions to be taken independently, even if this might seem to be the case for some Western business partners. Business decisions are joint decisions involving many representatives from the Japanese company in a laborious process.

7.4   Maintaining the business relationship

Even if the business in Japan goes well, good relationships cannot be taken for granted. Even if more negotiations are not anticipated in the near future, Japanese business people expect the relationship to be tended carefully. Greeting cards for Christmas, New Year and the summer festivals are very important in Japan and are supremely suitable as reminders and for showing deference to the Japanese partner. Ideally, there should be an annual trip to Japan to underpin the relationship even further.

Japanese business relationships are based on factors such as

- trust
- harmony and
- mutual obligation.

Before a business relationship with Japanese partners can even come into existence, a relationship of deep trust must develop between the future partners. Much time is invested in Japan to achieve the trust that is so important for true partnership (*shinyo*). It is important to get to know your opposite number as well as possible, both on a professional and on a private level and to find out more about his/her character. The search for trust explains the amalgamation of personal-private and business areas that is common in Japan. It also explains why the getting-to-know phase plays such an important role at the first meeting and why so much time is spent on seemingly irrelevant activities. Once a relationship of trust has developed, it requires careful tending to maintain it.

In all areas of society in Japan, group harmony (*wa*) is considered the ideal and must be achieved and maintained under all circumstances. Harmony is understood to include unity, accord, peace and quiet agreement in the interpersonal relationships in a group, which will achieve full potential only when harmony has been reached. The Japanese strive for harmony in business relationships so that consensus can be reached later on. Harmony and the resulting trust, loyalty and cooperation are considered factors for success in business and private relationships. Concern for group harmony leads individuals to avoid direct and open expressions of their opinion as far as possible (also see *honne* and *tatemae*). Confrontation of any kind must be avoided. However, that does not mean that there is no conflict in Japan, but that the way in which conflict is resolved is generally different from Western industrial countries.

The business relationship allows foreign partners to enter into trustful relationships with the Japanese but at the same time into a relationship of mutual obligation (*giri*) which plays a crucial role in the gift-giving tradition described above. Even if no visit to Japan is planned, gift packages from abroad as an expression of friendly obligation emphasize interest in the business relationship. The Japanese business partner might also expect, in return for previous favours, help in arranging private trips abroad, not only for himself/herself but also for friends and family members. Similarly, the foreign business partner can rely on support in matters that are equally of a private nature or which even diverge into additional areas of business. Long-lasting, perhaps even lifelong business relationships enjoy a very high social status in Japan and can represent definite competitive advantage for alternative strategies there.

Bibliography

Abegglen, J. C. and G. Stalk (1985) *Kaisha: The Japanese Corporation*. New York: Basic Books.

Abernathy, W., K. Clark and A. Kantrow (1981) "The New Industrial Competition", *Harvard Business Review*, 59, September–October, pp. 69–81.

Adler, P. S. (1988) "Managing Flexible Automation", *California Management Review*, 30(3 Spring), pp. 34–56.

American Chamber of Commerce (ACCJ) (2001) *Finding the Perfect Match: Recruiting, Developing, & Retaining Employees in Japan*. Unif: Price Water House Coopers.

Amyx, J. and P. Drysdale (eds) (2003) *Japanese Governance: Beyond Japan Inc.*, London: RoutledgeCurzon.

Anderson, O. (1997) "Internationalization and Market Entry Mode: A Review of Theories and Conceptual Frameworks", *Management International Review Studies*, 37 (special issue 2), S. 27–42.

Aoki, M. (1988) *Information, Incentives, and Bargaining in the Japanese Economy*. Cambridge: Cambridge University Press.

Aoki, M. (1989) "The Nature of the Japanese Firm as a Nexus of Employment and Financial Contracts: An Overview", *Journal of the Japanese International Economics*, 3, pp. 45–366.

Aoki, M. (1990) "Towards an Economic Model of the Japanese Firm", *Journal of Economic Literature*, 38(1), pp. 1–27.

Aoki, M. (1994) "The Japanese Firm as a System of Attributes: A Survey and Research Agenda", in M. Aoki, and R. Dore (eds) *The Japanese Firm. Source of Competitive Strength*, Oxford: Oxford University Press, pp. 11–40.

Aoki, M. (2000) *Information, Corporate Governance, and Institutional Diversity. Competitiveness in Japan, the USA, and the Transitional Economies*. Oxford: Oxford University Press.

Aoki, M. (2001) *Toward a Comparative Institutional Analysis*. Cambridge, MA: MIT Press.

Aoki, M. and R. Dore (1994) *The Japanese Firm: Sources of Competitive Strength*. New York: Oxford University Press.

Arai, S. and K. Bandlow (2005) "Japan-Engagement – Perspektiven für deutsche Unternehmen", in K. Bellmann and R. Haak (eds) *Management in Japan*. Herausforderungen und Erfolgsfaktoren für deutsche Unternehmen in einer dynamischen Umwelt. Wiesbaden, Gabler, pp. 31–48.

Argyris, C. and D. A. Schön (1978) *Organizational Learning. A Theory of Action Perspective*. Reading, MA: Addison-Wesley.

Argyris, C. and D. A. Schön (1999) *Die lernende Organisation*. Stuttgart: Klett-Cotta.

131

Arvey, R. D., R. S. Bhagat and E. Salas (1991) "Cross-Cultural and Cross National Issues in Personnel and Human Resource Management: Where do we go from here?", in G. R. Ferris and K. M. Rowland (eds) *Research in Personnel and Human Resource Management. A Research Annual*, 9, Greenwich, London: Jai Press, pp. 367–407.

Asakura, R. (2003) "The Androids Are Coming", *Japan Echo*, 30(4), pp. 13–18.

Asanuma, B. (1989) "Manufacturer-Supplier Relationships in Japan and the Concept of Relation-specific Skills", *Journal of the Japanese and International Economies*, 3, pp. 1–30.

Ballon, R. J. (1992) *Foreign Competition in Japan. Human Resource Strategies*. London, NY: Routledge.

Ballon, R. J. (2002) "Human Resource Management and Japan", *Euro Asia Journal of Management*, 12(1), pp. 5–20.

Ballon, R. J. (2005) "Organizational Survival", in R. Haak and M. Pudelko (eds) *Japanese Management – The Search for a New Balance Between Continuity and Change*, Houndmills, NY: Palgrave, pp. 55–77.

Ballon, R. J. and K. Honda (2000) *Stakeholding: The Japanese Bottom Line*. Tokyo: The Japan Times.

Ballon, R. J. and M. Matsuzaki (2000) *Japanese Business and Financial Disclosure*. Tokyo: Nikkei.

Bartlett, C. (1986) "Building and Managing the Transnational: The New Organizational Challenge", in M. Porter (ed.) *Competition in Global Industries*, Boston: Harvard Business School Press, pp. 367–401.

Bartlett, C. and S. Ghoshal (1989) *Managing Across Borders: The Transnational Solution*, Boston: Harvard Business School Press.

Bartlett, C. and S. Ghoshal (1990) "Matrix Management: Not a Structure, a Frame of Mind", *Harvard Business Review*, July–August, pp. 138–45.

Bartlett, C. and H. Yoshihara (1988) "New Challenges for Japanese Multinationals: Is Organizational Adaptation Their Achilles Heel?", *Human Resource Management*, 27, pp. 19–43.

Beason, R. and D. E. Weinstein (1994) "Growth, Economies of Scale, and Industrial Targeting in Japan (1955–1990)", *Harvard Institute of Economic Research Discussion Paper 1644*, Boston, June 10.

Beechler, S. and T. Iaquinto (1994) "A Longitudinal Study of Staffing Patterns in US Affiliates of Japanese Multinational Corporations", paper presented at the Association for Japanese Business Studies Annual Conference, January.

Beechler, S., J. Stephan, V. Pucik and N. Campbell (1995) "Decision Making Localization and Decentralization in Japanese MNCs: Are There Costs of Leaving Local Managers out of the Loop?", paper presented at the Academy of International Business Annual Conference, November.

Behrendt, W. K. (1982) "Die frühen Jahre der NC-Technologie: 1954 bis 1963", *Technische Rundschau*, 19, pp. 19–21.

Bellmann, K. and Haak, R. (eds) (2005) *Management in Japan*. Herausforderungen und Erfolgsfaktoren für deutsche Unternehmen in einer dynamischen Umwelt. Wiesbaden: Gabler.

Bleicher, K. (1982) "Japanisches Management im Wettstreit mit westlichen Kulturen", *Zeitschrift Führung & Organisation*, 51(7), pp. 444–50.

Bloom, H., R. Calori and P. de Wool (1994) *Euromanagement. A New Style for the Global Market*, London: Kogan Page.

Boesenberg, D. and H. Metzen (eds) (1993) *Lean Management. Vorsprung durch schlanke Konzepte*, Landsberg: Verlag Moderne Industrie.

BoJ (Bank of Japan) (2005) Monthly Report of Recent Economic and Financial Developments. 11/2005, Tokyo.

Bosse, F. (2000) "Keiretsu vor dem Aus?", *Japan aktuell, Wirtschaft, Politik, Gesellschaft* (April), pp. 139–46.

Boyacigiller, N. (1990a) "Staffing in a Foreign Land: A Multi-Level Study of Japanese Multinationals with Operations in the United States", presented at the Annual Academy of Management Conference, August.

Boyacigiller, N. (1990b) "The Role of Expatriates in the Management of Interdependence, Complexity, and Risk in Multinational Corporations", *Journal of International Business Studies*, 21(3), pp. 357–82.

Broda, C. and D. E. Weinstein (2004) "Happy News from the Dismal Science: Reassessing Japanese Fiscal Policy and Sustainability". Manuskript.

Brödner, P. (1991) "Maschinenbau in Japan – Nippons Erfolgskonzept: so einfach wie möglich", *Technische Rundschau*, 37, pp. 54–62.

Cabinet Office (2002) *Annual Report on the Japanese Economy and Public Finance 2001–2002: No Gains Without Reforms II*, Tokyo: Printing Bureau.

Cabinet Office (2004) Consumer Confidence Survey, March 2004.

Callen, T. and J. D. Ostry (eds) (2003) *Japan's Lost Decade: Policies for Economic Revival*. Washington, DC: International Monetary Fund.

Campbell, N. and N. Holden (eds) (1993) *Japanese Multinationals: Strategies and Management in the Global Kaisha*. London: Routledge.

Carroll, G. R. (1994) "The Specialist Strategy: Dynamics of Niche Width in Populations of Organizations", *American Journal of Sociology*, 90, pp. 126–283.

Chalmers, J. (1986) *MITI and the Japanese Miracle. The Growth of the Industrial Policy, 1925–1975*. Stanford: Stanford University Press.

Champy, J. and M. Hammer (1994) *Business Reengineering – Die Radikalkur für das Unternehmen*. Frankfurt and New York: Campus.

Chandler, A. (1990) *Scale and Scope. The Dynamics of Industrial Capitalism*. Cambridge: Belknap Press.

Chandler, A. (1992) Managerial Enterprise and Competitive Capabilities, *Business History*, 34, pp. 11–41.

Chang, C. S. (1982) "Individualism in the Japanese Management System", in S. M. Lee and G. Schwendiman (eds) *Japanese Management. Cultural and Environmental Considerations*, New York: Greenwood, pp. 82–8.

Chen, Z., M. Wakabayashi and N. Takeuchi (2004) "A Comparative Study of Organizational Context Factors for Managerial Career Progress: Focussing on Chinese State-Owned, Sino-Foreign Joint Ventures and Japanese Corporations", *International Journal of Human Resource Management*, 15(4), pp. 750–74.

Chokki, T. (1986) "A History of the Machine Tool Industry in Japan", in M. Fransman (ed.) *Machinery and Economic Development*, New York: St. Martin's Press, pp. 124–52.

Clark, K. B., T. Fujimoto and E. C. Stotko (eds) (1992) *Automobilentwicklung mit System. Strategie, Organisation und Management in Europa, Japan und USA.* Frankfurt am Main: Campus-Verlag.

Cole, R. E. (1972) "Permanent Employment in Japan: Fact and Fantasies", *Industrial and Labor Relations Review*, 26(1), pp. 615–30.

Colignon, R. A. and C. Usui (2003) *Amakudari: The Hidden Fabric of Japan's Economy.* Ithaca: Cornell University Press.

Collis, D. J. (1988) "The Machine Tool Industry and Industrial Policy 1955–1988", in M. E. Spence and H. A. Hazard (eds) *International Competitiveness*, Center of Business and Government at the John F. Kennedy School of Government, Harvard University, New York, pp. 75–114.

Conrad, H. and V. Gerling (2005) Der japanische "Silbermarkt"; – Marktchancen und Best Practies für deutsche Unternehmen, in K. Bellmann and R. Haak (eds) *Management in Japan*, Herausforderungen und Erfolgsfaktoren für deutsche Unternehmen in einer dynamischen Umwelt. Wiesbaden, Gabler, pp. 265–76.

Conrad, H. and S. Saaler (2001) Wohnen in Japan: Markt, Lebensformen, Wohnverhältnisse. In Japanstudien 13. iudicium Verlag, München, pp. 13–44.

Conrad, H. (2002a) Silver Market: Über die alternde Bevölkerung zu neuen Märkten, unveröffentlichtes Manuskript eines Vortrags auf der 9. Asien-Pazifik-Konferenz der Deutschen Wirtschaft. Unternehmerforum Japan. Tôkyô. 05.07.2002.

Conrad, H. (2002b) Die Pflegeversicherung in Japan: Hintergründe, Strukturen, Perspektiven, unveröffentlichtes Manuskript eines Vortrags beim Deutschen Zentrum für Altersfragen. Berlin. 20.11.2002.

Crawford, R. J. (1998) *Reinterpreting the Japanese Economic Miracle.* Cambridge, MA: Harvard University Press.

Dalton, N. and J. Benson (2002) "Innovation and Change in Japanese Human Resource Management", *Asia Pacific Journal of Human Resources*, 40(3), pp. 345–62.

Debroux, P. (2003) *Human Resource Management in Japan: Changes and Uncertainties. A New Human Resource Management Fitting to the Global Economy,* Aldershot: Ashgate.

Dentsu Center for Consumer Studies (2003) 2003 Hit Products in Japan. Towards a Freer Multidimensional Lifestyle – Six Different Moods to Create a Free, Vibrant Consumerism.

Dentsu Inc. (2004) 2003 Advertising Expenditures Classified by Industry.

Deutsches Institut für Japanstudien (ed.) (1998) *Die Wirtschaft Japans.* Berlin, Heidelberg, NY: Springer.

DIHKJ & Roland Berger Strategy Consultants (eds) (2003) *Making Money in Japan – Eine Studie zur Gewinnsituation deutscher Unternehmen in Japan.* Tokyo: DIHKJ.

DiMaggio, P. (ed.) (2001) *The Twenty-First Century Firm: Changing Economic Organization in International Perspective.* Princeton: Princeton University Press.

Dobson, H. and G. D. Hook (eds) (2003) *Japan and Britain in the Contemporary World: Responses to Common Issues*. London: RoutledgeCurzon.

Dore, R. (1973, 1990) *British Factory, Japanese Factory: The Origins of National Diversity in Industrial Relations*. London: Allen and Unwin, repr. University of California Press.

Dore, R. (1958, 2000) *City Life in Japan, A Study of a Tokyo Ward*, London: Routledge and Keagan Paul, repr. Curzon Press.

Dore, R. (1973) *British Factory – Japanese Factory*. Berkeley: University of California Press.

Dore, R. (1987) *Taking Japan Seriously. A Confucian Perspective on Leading Economic Issues*. Palo Alto: Stanford University Press.

Dore, R. (1990) *Will the 21st Century Be the Century of Individualism*. Tokyo: Simul Press.

Dore, R. (2000) *Stock Market Capitalism: Welfare Capitalism. Japan and Germany versus the Anglo-Saxons*. Oxford: Oxford University Press.

Dore, R. (2002) "Will Global Capitalism be Anglo-Saxon Capitalism?", *Asian Business & Management*, 1(1), pp. 9–18.

Doz, Y. L. (1986) *Strategic Management in Multinational Corporations*. Oxford: Pergamon Press.

Ducan, R. B. and A. Weiss (1979) "Organizational Learning: Implications for Organizational Design", in B. W. Staw (ed.) *Research in Organizational Behavior 1*, pp. 75–123.

Dunning, J. (1986) "Decision-Making Structures in US and Japanese Manufacturing Affiliates in the UK: Some Similarities and Contrasts", *Working Paper 41*, Geneva: International Labour Office.

Durand, J.-P., P. Stewart and J. J. Castillo (eds) (1999) *Teamwork in the Automobile Industry. Radical Change or Passing Fashion?* Houndsmill: Palgrave Macmillan.

Elder, M. (2003) "METI and Industrial Policy in Japan", in U. Schaede and W. Grimes (eds) *Japan's Managed Globalization: Adapting to the Twenty-first Century*, Armonk: Sharpe, pp. 159–90.

England, G. W. (1983) "Japanese and American Management: Beyond Theory Z", *Journal of International Business Studies*, 14(2), pp. 131–42.

Ernst, A. (1999) "Personnel Management of Japanese Firms and Information Flows", in H. Albach, U. Görtzen and R. Zobel (eds) *Information Processing as a Competitive Advantage of Japanese Firms*, Berlin: Edition Sigma, pp. 239–53.

Evans, P., V. Pucik and J. Barsoux (2002) *The Global Challenge: Frameworks for International Human Resource Management*. Boston, MA: McGraw-Hill Higher Education.

Fischer, W. (1979) *Die Weltwirtschaft im 20. Jahrhundert*. Göttingen: Vahlen.

Flath, D. (2000) "Japan's Business Groups", in M. Nakamura (ed.) *The Japanese Business and Economic System: History and Prospects for the 21st Century*, New York: Palgrave, pp. 281–324.

Ford, H. (1922) *My Life and Work*. New York: Doubleday & Page.

Foreign Press Center (2005) Japan Brief Nr. 0514: "China löst USA als wichtigsten Handelspartner Japans ab". Tokyo.

Foreign Press Center Japan (Hrsg.) (2004) *Facts and Figures of Japan 2004.* Tokyo: Foreign Press Center Japan.

Franko, L. (1973) "Who Manages Multinational Enterprises?", *Columbia Journal of World Business*, 8, pp. 30–42.

Freedman, D. (1988) *The Misunderstood Miracle – Industrial Development and Political Change in Japan.* London, Ithaca: Cornell University Press.

Freeman, J. (1995) "Business Strategy from the Population Level", in C. Montgomery (ed.) *Resource-Based and Evolutionary Theories of the Firm: Towards a Synthesis*, Boston, MA: Kluwer Academic Publishers.

Freeman, L. A. (2000) *Closing the Shop: Information Cartels and Japan's Mass Media.* Princeton: Princeton University Press.

Frenkel, S. (1994) "Pattern of Workplace Relations in the Global Corporation: Toward Convergence?", in J. Belanger, P. K. Edwards and L. Haiven (eds) *Workplace Industrial Relations and the Global Challenge*, Ithaca: ILR Press, pp. 210–74.

Freyssenet, M., A. Mair, K. Shimizu and G. Volpato (eds) (1998) *One Best Way? Trajectories and Industrial Models of the World's Automobile Producers.* Oxford, NY: Oxford University Press.

Fruin, W. M. (1992) *The Japanese Enterprise System: Competitive Strategies and Co-operative Structures.* Oxford: Clarendon.

Fujimoto, T. (1994) "Buhin Torihiki Kankei to Suparaiyâ Shisutemu" (Parts Transaction Relationships and the Supplier System), *Discussion Paper Series 94-J-19, Research Institute for the Japanese Economy*, Tokyo: The University of Tokyo Press.

Fujimoto, T. (1996) "An Evolutionary Process of Toyota's Final Assembly Operations. The Role of Ex-post Dynamic Capabilities", *Discussion Paper Series 96-F-2, Research Insitute for the Japanese Economy*, Tokyo: The University of Tokyo Press.

Fujimoto, T. (1999) *The Evolution of a Manufacturing System at Toyota.* Oxford and New York: Oxford University Press.

Fujimoto, T. and A. Takeishi (1994) *Jidôsha Sangyô 21 Seiki e no Shinario* (Scenario for the Car Industry in the 21st Century). Tokyo: Seisansei Shuppan.

Fujimoto, T., S. Sei and A. Takeishi (1994) Nihon Jidôsha Sangyô no Supuraiya Shisutemu no Zentaizô to sono Tamensei (The Whole Picture of the Supplier System of the Japanese Car Industry and its Diversity), *Kikai Keizai Kenkyû*, *24*, pp. 11–36.

Furin, W. E. and T. Nishiguchi (1990) The Toyota Production System. Its Organizational Definition in Japan, *Keizai Kenkyû*, 42(1), pp. 42–55.

Future Lifestyle Emphasis (2003) White Paper on Land, Infrastructure and Transport in Japan, 2002.

Gamble, J., J. Morris and B. Wilkinson (2004) "Mass Production is Alive and Well: The Future of Work and Organization in East Asia", *International Journal of Human Resource Management*, 15(2), pp. 397–409.

Garratt, B. (1990) *Creating a Learning Organisation. A Guide to Leadership, Learning and Development.* Cambridge: Director Books.

Geißler, H. (1996) "Vom Lernen in der Organisation zum Lernen der Organisation", in T. Sattelberger (ed.) *Die lernende Organisation: Konzepte für eine neue Qualität der Unternehmensentwicklung*, Wiesbaden: Gabler, pp. 79–95.

Gerling, V. and H. Conrad (2002) Wirtschaftskraft Alter in Japan: Handlungsfelder und Strategien. Unveröffentlichte Expertise im Auftrag des BMFSFJ. Dortmund, Tôkyô: Vervielfältigung.

Ghosn, C. (2002) "Saving the Business Without Losing the Company", *Harvard Business Review*, January, pp. 3–11.

Goetsch, D. L., and S. B. Davis (2003) *Quality Management: Introduction to Total Quality Management for Production, Processing, and Services*. Upper Saddle River, NJ: Prentice Hall.

Görgens, J. (1994) *Just in time Fertigung. Konzept und modellgestützte Analyse*. Stuttgart: Schäffer-Poeschel.

Griffin, G. C. (1955) "Maschinensteuerung – die Grundlage der Automatisierung", *Mach. shop. Mag.* 16, pp. 46–50.

Haak, R. (2000) "Kollektive Internationalisierungsstrategien der japanischen Industrie – Ein Beitrag zum Management Internationaler Unternehmungskooperationen", *Zeitschrift für wirtschaftlichen Fabrikbetrieb* (ZWF), 95(3), pp. 113–16.

Haak, R. (2001a) "Innovationen im Werkzeugmaschinenbau – Ein Überblick über die Frühphase der japanischen und deutschen Fertigungsautomatisierung", *Japan Analysen und Prognosen*, 175. Japan-Zentrum der Ludwig-Maximilians-Universität.: Munich.

Haak, R. (2001b) "Technologie und Management in Fernost – Ein Blick auf die Frühphase der japanischen Automatisierungstechnologie", *Zeitschrift für wirtschaftlichen Fabrikbetrieb* (ZWF), 96(5), pp. 274–80.

Haak, R. (2002) "Japanische Zuliefernetzwerke in der Globalisierung", *Zeitschrift für wirtschaftlichen Fabrikbetrieb* (ZWF), 97(3), pp. 133–6.

Haak, R. (2003) "Japanisches Produktionsmanagement", *Zeitschrift für wirtschaftlichen Fabrikbetrieb* (ZWF), 98(7/8), pp. 349–56.

Haak, R. (2003a) Japanisches Produktionsmanagement – Organisationales Lernen als strategischer Erfolgsfaktor. In: *Zeitschrift für wirtschaftlichen Fabrikbetrieb* (ZWF), Jahrgang 98, pp. 7–8.

Haak, R. (2003b) "A New Theoretical Approach to Internationalisation Strategies: First Thoughts About a Metastrategy", *Innovation: Management, Policy & Practice*, 5(1), September/October 2003, pp. 41–8.

Haak, R. (2003c) "Japanisches Produktionsmanagement – Organisationales Lernen als strategischer Erfolgsfaktor", *Zeitschrift für wirtschaftlichen Fabrikbetrieb* (ZWF), 98(2003) 7–8, pp. 67–73.

Haak, R. (2004a) "Japanese Supplier Network System in Transition – Survival Strategies", *Innovation: Management, Policy & Practice*, 6(1), pp. 45–9.

Haak, R. (2004b) *Theory and Management of Collective Strategies in International Business – The Impact of Globalization on Japanese-German Business Collaboration in Asia*. Basingstoke: Palgrave.

Haak, R. (2004c) *Theory and Management of Collective Strategies in International Business*. Houndsmill, Basingstoke, Hampshire, New York.

Haak, R. (2005) Japanese Production Management, in R. Haak, M. Pudelko (Hrsg.): *Japanese Management. The Search for a New Balance between Continuity and Change.* Houndsmill, Basingstoke, Hampshire, New York, pp. 213–40.

Haak, R. (ed.) (2006) The Changing Structure of Labour in Japan. Japanese Human Resource Management between Continuity and Innovation. Houndsmill, Basingstoke, Hampshire, New York.

Haak, R. and H. G. Hilpert (eds) (2003) *Focus China.* The New Challenge for Japanese Management. München, iudicium.

Haak, R. and M. Pudelko (eds) (2005) *Japanese Management – The Search for a New Balance Between Continuity and Change.* Houndsmills, Basingstoke, Hampshire: Palgrave Macmillan.

Haak, R. and D. Tachiki (eds) (2004) *Regional Strategies in a Global Economy.* Multinational Corporations in East Asia. München, iudicium.

Haak, U. (2001a) Der letzte Samurai, In: Die Zeit, http://www.zeit.de/archiv/ 2001/04/200104_kitano.xml.

Haak, U. (2001b) Du willst in die Hölle? Also bitte, geh doch! ZEIT-Gespräch mit Haruki Murakami In: Die Zeit, http://www.zeit.de/archiv/ 2001/13/200113_1-murakami_inter.xml.

Haak, U. (2001c) Japan: Sozialsysteme müssen umgebaut warden. In: Der Tagesspiegel vom 10.10.2001.

Haak, U. (2001d) Japanische Wirtschaft: Unternehmenskultur vor dem Umbruch. In: Der Tagesspiegel vom 10.09.2001.

Haak, U. (2001e) Post aus Japan: Es ist ein Mädchen. In: Der Tagesspiegel vom 02.12.2001.

Haak, U. (2002a) Post aus Japan: Kein Licht am Horizont. In: Der Tagesspiegel vom 03.02.2002.

Haak, U. (2002b) Post aus Tokio: Single-Frauen in Spendierhosen. In: Der Tagesspiegel vom 03.02.2002.

Haak, U. and R. Haak (2006) *Managerwissen kompakt: Japan.* München und Wien: Hanser.

Hakuhodo Inc. (2002) Hope. Hakuhodo Optimum Package for Elders. Tôkyô: Vervielfältigung.

Hakuhodo Inc. (2003) Hakuhodo Consumer Trend Report 2003. Un-Miserly Spending.

Hanft, A. (1996) "Organisationales Lernen und Macht – Über den Zusammenhang von Wissen, Lernen, Macht und Struktur", in G. Schreyögg and P. Conrad (eds) *Wissensmanagement,* Berlin and New York: de Gruyter, pp. 133–62.

Harzing, A. (1999) *Managing the Multinationals: An International Study of Control Mechanisms,* Cheltenham, UK: Edward Elgar.

Hayashi, S. (1991) *Culture and Management in Japan.* Tokyo: University of Tokyo Press.

Hayashi, M. (2002) "A Historical Review of Japanese Management Theories: The Search for a General Theory of Japanese Management", *Asian Business & Management,* 1(2), pp. 189–207.

Hayes, R. and W. Abernathy (1980) "Managing Our Way to Industrial Decline", *Harvard Business Review,* 58, July and August, pp. 69–77.

Hazama, H. (1997) *The History of Labour Management in Japan*. London: Macmillan.

Hemmert, M. and R. Lützeler (1994) "Einleitung: Landeskunde und wirtschaftliche Entwicklung seit 1945", *Die japanische Wirtschaft heute*. Miscellanea, Nr. 10, Tôkyô, DIJ, pp. 23–44.

Hirakubo, N. (1999) "The End of Lifetime employment in Japan", *Business Horizon*, 42(6), pp. 41–6.

Hirsch-Kreinsen, H. (1989) "Entwicklung einer Basistechnik. NC-Steuerung von Werkzeugmaschinen in den USA und der BRD", in K. Düll and B. Lutz (eds) *Technikentwicklung und Arbeitsteilung im internationalen Vergleich*, Munich: Hanser.

Hirsch-Kreinsen, H. (1993) *NC-Entwicklung als gesellschaftlicher Prozeß. Amerikanische und deutsche Innovationsmuster der Fertigungstechnik*. Frankfurt and New York: Campus-Verlag.

Hitachi Seki Kabushiki Kaisha: hito ni yasashii gijutsu – Chie to sôi no 55 nen – Sôritsu 55 shûnen (1991). (Hitachi Seki Co., Ldt. Menschenfreundliche Technologie – 55 Jahre Erfahrung und Kreativität, Schrift zum 55 jährigen Unternehmensbestehen). Tôkyô: Hitachi Seki.

Hoffmann, J. (1990) *Erfolgsbedingungen des Innovationsprozesses der numerisch gesteuerten Werkzeugmaschine in Japan*. Diplomarbeit. Berlin TU IWF.

Hofstede, G. (2001) *Culture's Consequences. Comparing Values, Behaviors, Institutions and Organizations across Nations*. (2nd ed), London, Thousand Oaks: Sage.

Holland, H. M. (1992) *Japan Challenges America: Managing an Alliance in Crisis*. Boulder: Westview Press.

Holtbrügge, D. (Hrsg.) (2003) *Management Multinationaler Unternehmungen*. Heidelberg: Physica-Verlag.

Horiuchi, K. and M. Nakamura (2000) "Environmental Issues and Japanese Firms", in M. Nakamura (ed.) *The Japanese Business and Economic System: History and Prospects for the 21st Century*, New York: Palgrave, pp. 364–84.

http://www.jetro.de/d/funde.pdf (Download 10.02.2006).

http://www.jetro.go.jp/en/market/trend/industrial/pdf/jem0509-2e2.pdf (Download 10.02.2006).

http://www.jetro.go.jp/en/market/trend/topic/2004_08_sapporo.html (Download 10.02.2006).

http://www.jetro.go.jp/en/market/trend/topic/2004_10_kobe.html (Download 10.02.2006).

http://www.jetro.go.jp/en/market/trend/topic/pdf/jem0507-topic2.pdf (Download 10.02.2006).

http://www.jetro.go.jp/en/market/trend/trend/2005_06_yokohama.html (Download 10.02.2006).

http://www.johotsusintokei.soumu.go.jp/whitepaper/eng/WP2005/2005-index.html (Download 10.02.2006).

http://www.kyoyohin.org/ Japan (gefunden am 04.08.2004).

http://www.kyoyohin.org/ Japan (gefunden am 04.08.2004).

http://www.mhlw.go.jp/english/database/db-hw/lifetb04/1.html   (Download 10.02.2006).
http://www.mlit.go.jp/english/ports/kowan3.html (Download 10.02.2006).
http://www.nenpuku.go.jp/yuusi/kinri.htlm#kinri1 (gefunden am 15.06.2001).
http://www1.ipss.go.jp/tohkei/Popular/Popular_f.html (gefunden am 31.07. 2004).
Huczynski, A. (1996) *Management Gurus. What Makes Them and How to Become One.* Boston: Thomson.
Hungenberg, H. (2002) Strategisches Management in Unternehmen – Ziele, Prozesse, Verfahren. Wiesbaden: Gabler.
Hyodo, T. (1987) "Participatory Management and Japanese Workers Consciousness", in J. Bergmann and S. Tokunaga (eds) *Economic and Social Aspects of Industrial Relations: A Comparison of the German and the Japanese Systems,* Frankfurt and New York: Campus-Verlag, pp. 261–70.
Ichimura, S. and K. Yoshihara (eds) (1985) "Japanese Management in Southeast Asia", *Southeast Asian Studies* 22 and 23, special issue.
Imai, K. (1989) "Evolution of Japans Corporate and Industrial Networks", in B. Carlsson (ed.) *Industrial Dynamics: Technological, Organizational, and Structural Changes in Industries and Firms,* Dordecht, Frankfurt am Main: Ullstein, pp. 123–55.
Imai, M. (1993) *Kaizen.* Frankfurt am Main: Ullstein.
Inohara, H. (1990) *Human Resource Development in Japanese Companies.* Tokyo: Asian Productivity Organization.
Itagaki, H. (2004) *Characteristics and Future of the Japanese Corporate Management System,* in Proceedings of the Euro-Asia Management Studies Association Annual Conference, Hong Kong, November 3–6.
Itô, T. (1992) *The Japanese Economy,* Cambridge, Mass. London: MIT Press.
Itoh, H. (1994) "Japanese Human Resource Management from the Viewpoint of Incentive Theory", in M. Aoki and R. Dore (eds) *The Japanese Firm: The Sources of Competitive Strength,* Oxford: Oxford University Press, pp. 233–64.
Jackson, G. (2003) "Corporate Governance in Germany and Japan: Liberalization Pressures and Responses during the 1990s", in K. Yamamura and W. Streeck (eds) *The End of Diversity? Prospects for German and Japanese Capitalism,* Ithaca: Cornell University Press, pp. 261–305.
JAMA (Japan Automobile Manufacturers Association) (2005) Active Matrix Database.
Japan Consumer Marketing Research Institute (2004) Consumer Trends and Marketing in Japan. A Look at the Essential Consumer Lifestyles.
Japan Labor Bulletin (2002a) "Number of Firms and Regular Employees Down; Number of Part-Time and Temporary Workers Up", 41(10), p. 3.
Japan Labor Bulletin (2002b) "Only Half of Granted Holidays Actually Taken", 42(1), p. 2.
Japan Labor Bulletin (2003) "Unionization Rate Drops to Record Low 20, 2 Percent", 42(3), p. 4.

Japanese Institute of Labour (JIL) (1998) *Japanese Working Life Profile*. Tokyo: Japanese Institute of Labour.

JETRO (1992) *Nippon 1992 Facts and Figures*. Tokyo: Japan External Trade Organization.

JETRO (2000) Japanese Market Report No. 50 – Senior Citizen-related Businesses. JETRO.

JETRO (2004a) http://www.jetro.go.jp/ecle/articles/changing/docs/2004_01_fdi.html (Download January 15, 2004).

JETRO (2004b) Guide to Business Opportunities in Japan – Environmental Market. Tokyo.

JETRO (2004c) Trends and Topics, Business Topics: "Japan's Regional Clusters (1): Sapporo Valley".

JETRO (2004c) Trends and Topics, Business Topics: "Japan's Regional Clusters (3): Kobe Medical Industry City".

JETRO (2005a) 10 Advantages to Investing in Japan. Tokyo.

JETRO (2005b) Attractive Sectors: Automotive Parts. Tokyo.

JETRO (2005c) Attractive Sectors: Biotechnology. Tokyo.

JETRO (2005d) Attractive Sectors: Environment. Tokyo.

JETRO (2005e) Attractive Sectors: ICT – Information and Communication Technology. Tokyo.

JETRO (2005f) Attractive Sectors: Medical Care. Tokyo.

JETRO (2005g) Japanese Market Report No. 76: "Automobile Assembly Parts". Tokyo.

JETRO (2005h) Trends and Topics, Industrial Report: "Networked Home Appliances in Japan".

JETRO (2005i) Trends and Topics, Business Topics: "Japan's Changing Medical Care Scene".

JETRO (2005j) Trends and Topics, Regional Trends: "Japan's Regional Clusters – Yokohama the City of Life Sciences".

JETRO (2006) Trends and Topics, Special Reports: "Japanese R&D Draws More Attention" http://www.jetro.go.jp/en/market/trend/special/pdf/jem0511-1e.pdf.

JETRO München (2005) Japan als Standort für Forschung und Entwicklung.

JETRO and JMA (JMA Research Institute) (2005) Market Survey for Investment in Japan – Subject Fields: Environment. Tokyo.

JETRO and MRI (Mitsubishi Research Institute) (2005) Market Survey for Investment in Japan – Subject Fields: ICT. Tokyo.

JETRO and NRI (Nomura Research Institute) (2005) Market Survey for Investment in Japan – Subject Fields: Medical and Welfare. Tokyo.

JETRO and Yano (Yano Research Institute Ltd.) (2005) Market Survey for Investment in Japan – Subject Fields: Bio Technology. Tokyo.

JFTC (Japan Fair Trade Commission) (1995) *Report on Economic Concentration*, Tokyo.

JFTC (Japan Fair Trade Commission) (1996) *Annual Report on Competition Policy in Japan (January–December 1995)*, Tokyo.

JFTC (Japan Fair Trade Commission) (2001) *State of Corporate Groups in Japan: The 7th Survey Report*, Tokyo.

Johnson, R. (1977) "Success and Failure of Japanese Subsidiaries in America", *Columbia Journal of World Business* 12, pp. 30–7.

Johnson, C. (1982) *MITI and the Japanese Miracle. The Growth of Industrial Policy 1925–1975*, Stanford: Stanford University Press.

JSBRI (Japan Small Business Research Institute) (2002) *White Paper on Small and Medium Enterprises in Japan. The Age of the Local Entrepreneur – Birth, Growth and Revitalization of the National Economy*, Tokyo.

JSBRI (Japan Small Business Research Institute) (2003) *White Paper on Small and Medium Enterprises in Japan. The Road to Reorganization and the Creation of an Entrepreneurial Society*, Tokyo.

Jung, H. F. (1992) Lean-Management. Arbeitswelt und Unternehmensethik in Japan in: Lean-Management. Ideen für die Praxis. *Dokumentation einer Informations – und Diskussionsreihe* (WiSo-Führungskräfte-Akademie Nürnberg), pp. 102–30.

Jürgens, U. (1991) *Kaizen – die Organisation von Verbesserungsaktivitäten zwischen Industrial Engineering und Qualitätszirkelaktivitäten*, Wissenschaftszentrum Berlin, Berlin.

Jürgens, U. (1994) "Lean Production", in H. Corsten (ed.) *Handbuch Produktionsmanagement*, Wiesbaden: Gabler, pp. 369–79.

Jürgens, U. (2003) "Transformation and Interaction: Japanese, U.S., and German Production Models in the 1990s", in K. Yamamura and W. Streeck (eds) *The End of Diversity? Prospects for German and Japanese Capitalism*, Ithaca: Cornell University Press, pp. 212–39.

Jürgens, U., T. Malsch and K. Dohse (1989) *Moderne Zeiten in der Automobilfabrik. Strategie der Produktmodernisierung im Länder- und Konzernvergleich*, Berlin, Heidelberg and New York: Springer.

Kanter, R. M. (1991) "Transcending Business Boundaries: 12,000 World Managers View Change", *Harvard Business Review*, 69, pp. 151–64.

Kanter, R. M. (1995) *World Class: Thriving Locally in the Global Economy*. New York: Simon and Schuster.

Katzenstein, P. J. (2003) "Regional States: Japan and Asia, Germany in Europe", in K. Yamamura and W. Streeck (eds) *The End of Diversity? Prospects for German and Japanese Capitalism*, Ithaca: Cornell University Press, pp. 89–114.

Keizai Kikakuchô (1994) *Kokumin keizai keisan nenpô (Annual report on National Accounts)*, Tôkyô, Keizai Kikakuchô keizai Kenkyujo, pp. 46–7.

Keizai Sangyôshô (2002) 2000-nendo ni okeru fukushi yôgu shijô kibo suikei ni tsuite [Zur Schätzung der Größe des Marktes für Pflegeprodukte im Fiskaljahr 2000]. Tôkyô: Keizai Sangyôshô.

Kennedy, P. (1954) "Automatic Controls Takes Over in Automotive Manufacturing", *Automotive Industry*, 111, pp. 62–7 and pp. 138–44.

Kenney, M. and R. Florida (1988) "Beyond Mass Production: Production and the Labour Process in Japan", *Politics and Society*, 16(1), pp. 121–58.

Kenney, M. and R. Florida (1993) *Beyond Mass Production: The Japanese System and its Transfer to the US.* Oxford: Oxford University Press.

Kief, H. B. (1991) "Von der NC zur CNC: Die Entwicklung der numerischen Steuerungen", *Werkstatt und Betrieb*, 124(5), pp. 385–91.

Kim, W. C. and A. Mauborgne (1996) "Procedural Justice and Managers" In-role and Extra-role Behavior: The Case of the Multinational', *Management Science*, 42, pp. 499–515.

Kobayashi, N. (1982) "The Present and Future of Japanese Multinational Enterprises: A Comparative Analysis of Japanese and US-European Multinational Management", *International Studies of Management and Organization*, 12, pp. 38–58.

Kobayashi, N. (1985) "The Patterns of Management Style Developing in Japanese Multinationals in the 1980s", in S. Takamiya and K. Thurley (eds) *Japan's Emerging Multinationals*, Tokyo: University of Tokyo Press, pp. 229–64.

Kobayashi, K. (1996) Business mit Japan. München, Wirtschaftsverlag Langen Müller Herbig.

Kobrin, S. J. (1994) "Is There a Relationship Between a Geocentric Mind-Set and Multinational Strategy?", *Journal of International Business Studies*, 25, pp. 493–511.

Koike, K. (1997) "Human Resource Development", *Japanese Economy and Labour Series*, no. 2, Tokyo: Japanese Institute of Labour.

Kokudo Kôtsûshô (2001) Hôritsu no kaisei nado [Gesetzesrevisionen und anderes]. http.//www.mlit.go.jp/jutakukentiku/house/torikumi/koureishahou-gaiyou.htm (gefunden am 15.06.2001).

Kokuritsu Shakai Hoshô Jinkô Mondai Kenkyûjo (2004) Ippan jinkô tôkei – jinkô tôkei shiryôshu – Heisei 14-nenpan [Allgemeine Bevölkerungsstatistik 2003]

Kono, T. and S. Clegg (2001) *Trends in Japanese Management. Continuing Strengths, Current Problems and Changing Priorities*, Houndmills, NY: Palgrave.

Kopp, R. (1999) "The Rice-Paper Ceiling in Japanese Companies: Why it Exists and Persists", in S. Beechler and A. Bird (eds) *Japanese Multinationals Abroad: Individual and Organizational Learning*, New York: Oxford University Press, pp. 107–28.

Koshiro, K. (1994) The Employment System and Human Resource Management, in K. Imai and R. Koyama (eds) *Business Enterprises in Japan – Views of leading Japanese economists,* Cambridge, Massachusetts, London: MIT Press, pp. 247–9.

Koshiro, K. (2000) *A Fifty Year History of Industry and Labor in Postwar Japan.* Japanese Economy & Labor Series no. 6, Tôkyô: The Japan Institute of Labor.

Kostova, T. and K. Roth (2003) "Social Capital in Multinational Corporations and a Micro-Macro Model of its Formation", *Academy of Management Review*, 28(2), pp. 297–329.

Kriger, M. and E. Solomon (1992) "Strategic Mindsets and Decision-Making Autonomy in US and Japanese MNCs", *Management International Review*, 32(4), pp. 327–43.

Kutschker, M. and S. Schmid (2002) *Internationales Management*. München, Wien: Oldenbourg.

Kyôyo-Hin Foundation (2004) Kyôyo-Hin Foundation, Japan.

Lawrence, P. R. and J. W. Lorsch (1967) *Organization and Environment*, Cambridge, MA: Harvard University Press.

Lebow, D. (2004) The monetisation of Japan's government debt. BIS (Bank for International Settlements) Working Paper No. 161.

Lee, S.-H. (2000) Erfolgreiches Asienmanagement: China/Hongkong – Japan, Renningen-Malmsheim, expert-Verlag.

Leme Fleury, M. T. (1996) "Managing Human Resources for Learning and Innovation: A Comparative Study of Brazilian, Japanese and Korean Firms", *International Journal for Human Resource Management*, 7(4), pp. 797–812.

Levy, O. (2003) "The Influence of Top Management Team Global Mindset on Global Strategic Posture of Firms", unpublished working paper.

Ley, A. (2000) Silberindustrie: Geschäft mit dem Altwerden. In: Japan Magazin 9/00, S. 16–25.

Liker, J. K. (ed.) (1997) *Becoming Lean: Inside Stories of U.S. Manufactures*, Portland, OR: Productivity Press.

Liker, J. K. (2004) *The Toyota Way*, New York: MacGraw-Hill.

Lincoln, E. J. (2001) *Arthritic Japan: The Slow Pace of Economic Reform*, Washington, DC: Brookings Institution Press.

Lincoln, J. R. (1989) "Employee Work Attitudes and Management Practices in the U.S. and Japan: Evidence from a Large Comparative Survey", *California Management Review*, 32(1), pp. 89–106.

Lux, W. (1997) "Japanese Management Evolves Again", *Management Review*, 86(6), pp. 36–9.

Macharzina, K. and M.-J. Oesterle (Hrsg.) (2002) Hanbuch Internationales Management: Grundlagen – Instrumente – Perspektiven. Wiesbaben, Gabler.

Magota, R. (1970) *Nenko-Chingin no Ayumi to Mirai-Chingin Taikei 100 Nen-shi* [The past and future of the seniority wage system – 100 years of the Japanese wage system], Sangyo R Chosa-sho.

Manpower Services Commission (MSN) (1987) *The Making of Managers. A Report on Management Education, Training and Development in the USA, West Germany, France, Japan and the UK*. National Economic Development Council and British Institute of Management: London.

Maruyama, H. (2004) Omron Eyes All-time High Net Profit – Control Equipment Maker's Command of Local Market Keeps Sales Humming Nikkei Weekly. Nihon Keizai Shimbun, 22 March, p. 24.

Maslow, A. H. (1954) *Motivation and Personality*. New York: Harper.

Matanle, P. (2003) *Japanese Capitalism and Modernity in a Global Era. Re-fabricating Lifetime Employment Relations*. London, NY: RoutledgeCurzon.

Matzky, U. (1994) "Das Management des kontinuierlichen Verbesserungsprozesses in der japanischen Automobilindustrie", in Ostasiatisches Seminar der Freien Universität Berlin (eds) *Soziale und Wirtschaftliche Studien über Japan/Ostasien. Occasional Paper,* 91.

Maurer, J. (2004a) Unternehmen und Regierung setzen auf E-Japan. Japanmarkt. November, S. 6–9.

Maurer, J. (2004b) Cluster sollen industrielle Basis stärken. Japanmarkt, Dezember S. 12–15.

Maurer, J. (2005a) Japans Wirtschaft zum Jahreswechsel auf Konsolidierungskurs. Japanmarkt. Januar, S. 6–17.

Maurer, J. (2005b) Japans Trendsucher sehen für 2005 gute Konsumbasis. Japanmarkt. Februar, S. 6–7.

Maurer, J. (2005c) Lifestyle und Konsum in Japan. in K. Bellmann and R. Haak (Hrsg.) *Management in Japan.* Herausforderungen und Erfolgsfaktoren für deutsche Unternehmen in einer dynamischen Umwelt, Wiesbaden, Gabler, S. 257–264.

McLeod, R. H. and R. Garnaut (1998) (eds) *East Asia in Crisis: From Being a Miracle to Needing One?* London: Routledge.

McMillan, C. J. (1996) *The Japanese Industrial System.* (2nd ed), Berlin, New York: Walter de Gruyter.

Meierhans, Ingo und Flock, Christian (2004) Wie wettbewerbsfähig ist Japan. In: Pohl, Manfred und Iris Wieczorek (Hrsg.) *Japan 2004 – Politik und Wirtschaft.* Hamburg: Institut für Asienkunde, S. 167–189.

Methe, D. (2005) "Continuity Through Change in Japanese Management: Institutional and Strategic Influences", in R. Haak and M. Pudelko (eds) *Japanese Management – The Search for a New Balance between Continuity and Change,* Houndmills, New York: Palgrave, pp. 21–54.

MHLW (Ministry of Health, Labor and Welfare) (2004) Life expectancy at specific ages.

MIC (Ministry of Internal Affairs and Communications) (2005) Information and Communications in Japan, White Paper 2005: Stirrings of u-Japan.

Ministry of Public Management, Home Affairs, Posts and Telecommunications (2004) Information and Communications in Japan 2004. Building a Ubiquitous Network Society That Spreads Throughout the World.

MOF (Ministry of Finance) (2005) Foreign Direct Investment. http://www.mof. go.jp/ english/e1c008.htm (Download 10.02.2006).

Mommertz, K. H. (1981) *Bohren, Drehen und Fräsen. Geschichte der Werkzeugmaschinen.* Reinbek bei Hamburg.

Monden, Y. (1983) *Toyota Production System.* Norcross, Ga.: Industrial Engineering and Management Press.

Morgan, G., B. Kelley and R. Whitley (2003) "Global Managers and Japanese Multinationals: Internationalization and Management in Japanese Financial Institutions", *International Journal of Human Resource Management,* 14(3), pp. 389–407.

Morikawa, H. (2001) *A History of Top Management in Japan: Managerial Enterprises and Family Enterprises.* Oxford: Oxford University Press.

Morishima, M. (1995a) "Embedding HRM in a Social Context", *British Journal of Industrial Relations*, 33(4), pp. 617–640.

Morishima, M. (1995b) "The Japanese Human Resource Management System: A Learning Bureaucracy", in L. Moore and P. Jennings (eds) *Human Resource Management on the Pacific Rim. Institutions, Practices, and Attitudes*, Berlin, New York: Walter de Gruyter, pp. 119–150.

Morishima, M. (2000) "A Break with Tradition: Negotiating New Psychological Contracts in Japan", in D. M. Rousseau and R. Schalk (eds) *Psychological Contracts in Employment: Cross-National Perspectives*, Thousand Oaks: Sage Publications, pp. 141–157.

Morishima, M. (2003) "Changes in White-Collar Employment from the Employee's Perspective", *Japan Labour Bulletin*, 42(9), pp. 8–19.

Moss-Kanter, R. (1991) "Transcending Business Boundaries: 12,000 World Managers View Change", *Harvard Business Review* May/June, pp. 151–164.

Muramatsu, M., F. Iqbal and I. Kume (eds) (2001) *Local Government Development in Post-war Japan*, Oxford: Oxford University Press.

Nahapiet, J. and S. Ghoshal (1998) "Social Capital, Intellectual Capital, and the Organizational Advantage", *Academy of Management Review*, 23, pp. 242–266.

Nakamura, K. (1993) *Subcontracting System and Segmented Labour Market in Japan*. Musashi Universtity, Tokyo.

Nakamura, T. (1996) *Lectures on Modern Japanese Economic History 1926–1994*. Tôkyô: The Universtiy of Toyko Press.

Nakamura, K. (2000) "Localization of Management in Japanese-related Firms in Indonesia". www.jetro.go.jp/bulletin 39-07.

Nakamura, M. (ed.) (2000) *The Japanese Business and Economic System: History and Prospects for the 21st Century*. New York: Palgrave.

Nakane, C. (1970) *Japanese Society*. Berkeley: University of California Press.

National Institute of Population and Social Security Research (2000). Population Projections for Japan: 2001–2050.

National Tax Administration (1991) *Hôjin Kigyô no Jittai Heisei 3-Nenbun* [Actual Situation of Juridical Entity Enterprises, Annual 1990], Tokyo.

National Tax Administration (2002) *Hôjin Kigyô no Jittai Heisei 12-Nenbun* [Actual Situation of Juridical Entity Enterprises, Annual 2000], Tokyo.

Negandhi, A. and B. Baliga (1979) *Quest for Survival and Growth: A Comparative Study of American, European, and Japanese Multinationals*. New York: Praeger Publishers.

Negandhi, A. and B. Baliga (1981a) "Internal Functioning of American, German and Japanese Multinational Corporations", in L. Otterbeck (ed.) *The Management of Headquarters-Subsidiary Relationships in Multinational Corporations*, New York: St. Martin's Press, pp. 107–120.

Negandhi, A. and B. R. Baliga (1981b) *Tables are Turning: German and Japanese Multinational Companies in the United States*. Cambridge, MA: Oelgeschlager, Gunn & Hain Publishers, Inc.

Negandhi, A., G. Eshghi and E. Yuen (1985) "The Management Practices of Japanese Subsidiaries Overseas", *California Management Review*, 27, pp. 83–105.

Nenkin Shikin Un'yô Kikin (2001) Nenkin jûtaku yûshin [Baufinanzierung des Government Pension Investment Fonds].

Nihon Kôsaku Kikai Kôgyôkai (1982) *Haha-naru kikai: 30 nen no ayumi* [Japan Machine Tool Builders Association, The Mother of Machines: Thirty Years of History], Tokyo: Nihon Kôsaku Kikai Kôgyôkai, pp. 81–83.

Nihon Noritsu Kyokai (1978) *Toyota no Genba Kanri*. Tokyo: Nihon Noritsu Kyokai.

Nihon Zaigai Kigyo Kyokai (1987) *Firipin ni okeru nikkei kigyo to sono kankyo: Anketo chosa genchi chosa kekka hokokusho*. Tokyo: Nihon Zaigai Kigyo Kyokai.

Nikkei Weekly (2004a) Consumers looking past price tags. In: Nikkei Weekly, July 5.

Nikkei Weekly (2004b) New products get a woman's touch. In: Nikkei Weekly, June 28.

Nikkei Weekly (28.06.2004) Designs enhance user-friendliness of home care, S. 19.

Noble, G. W. (2003) "Reform and Continuity in Japan's *Shingikai* Deliberation Councils", in J. Amyx and P. Drysdale (eds) (2003) *Japanese Governance: Beyond Japan Inc.*, London: RoutledgeCurzon, pp. 113–133.

Nonaka, I. (1988) "Towards Middle-Up-Down Management: Accelerating Information Creation", *Sloan Management Review*, pp. 9–18.

Nonaka, I. (1990) "Redundant, Overlapping Organization: A Japanese Approach to Managing the Innovation Process", *California Management Review* 32(3), pp. 27–38.

Nonaka, I. and H. Takeuchi (1995) *The Knowledge-Creating Company: How Japanese Companies Create the Dynamics of Innovation*. Oxford: Oxford University Press.

Nonaka, I. and H. Takeuchi (1997) *Die Organisation des Wissens. Wie japanische Unternehmen eine brachliegende Ressource nutzbar machen*. Frankfurt am Main, New York: Campus-Verlag.

O'Reilly, C. A. and J. A. Chatman (1986) "Organizational Commitment and Psychological Attachment: The Effects of Compliance, Identification, and Internalization on Prosocial Behavior", *Journal of Applied Psychology* 71, pp. 492–499.

Oda, H. (1992) *Japanese Law*. London: Butterworths.

Odagiri, H. (1992) *Growth through Competition, Competition through Growth. Strategic Management and the Economy in Japan*. Oxford: Oxford University Press.

Odaka, K. and M. Sawai (eds) (1999) *Small Firms, Large Concerns: The Development of Small Business in Comparative Perspective*. Oxford: Oxford University Press.

OECD (Organisation for Economic Co-operation and Development) (2000) *OECD Economic Surveys 1999–2000: Japan*, Paris.

OECD (Organisation for Economic Co-operation and Development) (2003) *OECD Economic Surveys 2001–2002: Japan*, Paris.

OECD (Organisation for Economic Co-operation and Development) (2004) *OECD Economic Surveys 2003–2004: Japan,* Paris.

Ohno, T. (1978) *Toyota Production System: Beyond Large-Scale Production.* Cambrigde: Productivity Press.

Ohtsu, M. and T. Iwanari (2002) *Inside Japanese Business: A Narrative History, 1960-2000.* Armonk: Sharpe.

Okabe, M. (2002) *Cross Shareholdings in Japan: A New Unified Perspective of the Economic System.* Cheltenham: Edward Elgar.

Okabe, Y. (2002) "Culture or Employment Systems? Accounting for the Attitudinal Differences between British and Japanese Managers", *International Journal of Human Resource Management* 13(2), pp. 285–301.

Okumura, H. (2000) *Corporate Capitalism in Japan.* New York: St. Martin's Press.

Organization for Economic Cooperation and Development (1991) *OECD Economic Surveys: Japan,* New York: OECD.

Ornatowski, G. (1998) "The End of Japanese-Style Human Resource Management", *Sloan Management Review* 39(3), pp. 73–84.

Ouchi, W. (1981) *Theory Z: How American Business Can Meet the Japanese Challenge.* Reading: Addison-Wesley.

Ouchi, W. G. and J. B. Johnson (1978) "Types of Organizational Control and Their Relationship to Emotional Well Being", *Administrative Science Quarterly* 23(2), pp. 293–317.

Park, S.-J. (1975) "Die Wirtschaft seit 1868", in H. Hammitz (ed.) *Japan,* Nuremberg, pp. 123–144.

Park, S.-J. (1985) "Informalismus als Managementrationalität", in S.-J. Park (ed.)*Japanisches Management in der Praxis. Flexibilität oder Kontrolle im Prozess der Internationalisierung und Mikroelektronisierung,* Berlin: Express Edition, pp. 101–118.

Park, S.-J. (ed.) (1985) *Japanisches Management in der Praxis: Flexibilität oder Kontrolle im Prozess der Internationalisierung und Mikroelektronisierung.* Berlin: Express Edition.

Parker, M. und Slaughter, J. (1988) *Choosing Sides: Union and Team Concept.* Boston: South End Press.

Pascal, R. T. and A. G. Athos (1981) *The Art of Japanese Management.* Harmondsworth: Penguin Books Limited.

Pascha, W (2003) "Wirtschaft", in P. Kevenhörster, W. Pascha and Shire, Karen A. (eds) Japan. Wirtschaft, Gesellschaft, Politik, Opladen, Leske+Budrich, S. 15–178.

Pascha, W. (2005) "Japan als Standort in Asien: Regionale Konfigurationsentscheidungen aus deutscher Sicht." in K. Bellmann and R. Haak (Hrsg.) *Management in Japan.* Herausforderungen und Erfolgsfaktoren für deutsche Unternehmen in einer dynamischen Umwelt, Wiesbaden, Gabler, S. 71–88.

Pascha, W. (2006) *Gesamtwirtschaftliche Megatrends in Japan und ihre Implikationen für die Industriestruktur.* Erscheint in: Institut für Asienstudien: *Japan aktuell.* Hamburg.

Patrick, H. (ed.) (1976) *Japanese Industrialization and Its Social Consequences.* Berkeley: University of California Press.

Patrick, H. (2003) "Comment", in R. M. Stern (ed.) *Japan's Economic Recovery: Commercial Policy, Monetary Policy, and Corporate Governance,* Cheltenham: Edward Elgar, pp. 329–334.

Penrose, E. (1959) *The Theory of the Growth of the Firm.* Oxford: Oxford University Press.

Perlitz, M. (1997) "Spektrum kooperativer Internationalisierungsformen," in K. Marcharzina and M.-J. Oesterle (Hrsg.) *Handbuch Internationales Management,* Wiesbaden, Gabler S. 441–457.

Perlitz, M. and Seger, F. (2000) "Konzepte internationaler Markteintrittsstrategien," in D. von der Oelsnitz (Hrsg.) *Markteintrittsmanagement. Probleme, Strategien, Erfahrungen.* Stuttgart, Schäffer-Poeschel, S. 89–110,.

Perlmutter, H. (1969) "The Tortuous Evolution of the Multinational Corporation", *Columbia Journal of World Business* January–February, pp. 9–18.

Perlmutter, H. and D. Heenan (1979) *Multinational Organization Development,* Reading, MA: Addison-Wesley.

Peters, T. J. and R. H. Waterman (1982) In Search of Excellence. New York: Harper & Row.

Pfeiffer, W. and E. Weiß (eds) (1990) *Technologie-Management.* Göttingen: Vandenhoeck & Ruprecht.

Pilling D. and M. Nakamoto (2004) *Japan Chooses Cosmetic Change.* Financial Times, 5 March, p. 8.

Plenert, G. J. (1990) *International Management and Production. Survival Techniques for Corporate America.* New York: MacGraw-Hill.

Porter, M. (1990) *The Competitive Advantage of Nations.* New York: Free Press.

Porter, M. E., H. Takeuchi and M. Sakakibara (2000) *Can Japan Compete?* Cambridge, Mass.: Perseus.

Porter, M., H. Takeuchi and M. Sakakibara (2000) *Can Japan Compete?* London: Macmillan.

Prahalad, C. K. and G. Hamel (1994) "Strategy as a Field of Study: Why Search for a New Paradigm?", *Strategic Management Journal* 15, pp. 5–16.

Pucik, V. (1999) "Where Performance Does not Matter: Human Resource Management in Japanese-Owned US Affiliates", in S. Beechler and A. Bird (eds) *Japanese Multinationals Abroad: Individual and Organizational Learning,* New York: Oxford University Press, pp. 169–188.

Pucik, V., M. Hanada and G. Fifield (1989) *Management Culture and the Effectiveness of Local Executives in Japanese-owned US Corporations.* Ann Arbor, MI: The University of Michigan and Egon Zehnder.

Pucik, V., N. Tichy and C. Barnett (eds) (1992) *Globalizing Management: Creating and Leading the Competitive Organization.* New York: John Wiley & Sons.

Pudelko, M. (2000a–c) *Das Personalmanagement in Deutschland, den USA und Japan. Vol. 1: Die gesamtgesellschaftlichen Rahmenbedingungen im Wettbewerb der Systeme; vol. 2: Eine systematische und vergleichende Bestandsaufnahme; vol. 3: Wie wir voneinander lernen können.* Köln: Saborowski.

Pudelko, M. (2004a) "HRM in Japan and the West: What are the Lessons to Be Learnt from Each Other?", *Asian Business and Management*, 3(3), pp. 337–61.

Pudelko, M. (2004b) "Benchmarking: Was amerikanische, japanische und deutsche Personalmanager voneinander lernen", *Zeitschrift für Personalforschung*, 18(2), pp. 139–63.

Purcell, W., S. Nicholas and D. Merrett (1998) "The Transfer of Human Resource Management Practice by Japanese Multinationals to Australia: Does Industry, Size and Experience Matter?", *Discussion Paper No. 5*, Australian Centre for International Business.

Ramseyer, J. M. (1986) "Lawyers, Foreign Lawyers, and Lawyers Substitutes: The Market for Regulation in Japan", *Harvard International Law Journal*, 27, p. 124.

Ramseyer, J. M. (2000) "Rational Litigant Redux: A Response to Professor Hamada", in M. Aoki and G. R. Saxonhouse (eds) *Finance, Governance, and Competitiveness in Japan*, Oxford: Oxford University Press, pp. 195–98.

Ramseyer, J. M. and M. Nakazato (1998) *Japanese Law: An Economic Approach*. Chicago: University of Chicago Press.

Robinson, R. (1985) *The Japan Syndrome: Is there One?* Atlanta, GA: CBA.

Rossmann, U. (2005) Anpassungen vertikaler Keiretsu-Strukturen in Japan, in K. Bellmann and R. Haak (Hrsg.) Management in Japan, Herausforderungen und Erfolgsfaktoren für deutsche Unternehmen in einer dynamischen Umwelt, Wiesbaden, Gabler, S. 277–94.

Rousseau, D. M. and R. Schalk (eds) (2000) *Psychological Contracts in Employment: Cross-National Perspectives*, Thousand Oaks: Sage Publications.

Rowley, C., J. Benson and M. Warner (2004) "Towards an Asian Model of Human Resource Management? A Comparative Analysis of China, Japan and South Korea", *International Journal of Human Resource Management*, 15(5), pp. 917–33.

Sano, Y. (1993) "Changes and Continued Stability in Japanese HRM Systems: Choice in the Share Economy", *International Journal of Human Resource Management*, 4(1), pp. 11–27.

Schaede, U. (2000) *Co-operative Capitalism: Self-Regulation, Trade Associations, and the Antimonopoly Law in Japan*. Oxford: Oxford University Press.

Schaede, U. and W. Grimes (eds) (2003) *Japan's Managed Globalization: Adapting to the Twenty-first Century*. Armonk: Sharpe.

Scherm, M. and P. R. Bischoff (1994) "Lean Management – stereotype Sichtweisen japanischer Unternehmensphänomene", in M. Esser and K. Kobayashi (eds) *Kaishain. Personalmanagement in Japan. Sinn und Werte statt Systeme, Psychologie für das Personalmanagement*, Göttingen: Verl. für Angewandte Psychologie, pp. 100–107.

Schmitt, W. W. (1998) *Management japanischer Niederlassungen. Strukturen und Strategien*. Bonn: Institut für Wissenschaftliche Publikationen.

Schneidewind, D. (1997) *Markt und Marketing in Japan*. München, Verlag C. H. Beck.

Schröder, S. (1995) *Innovation in der Produktion*. Berlin: IPK Berlin.

Schüle, U. "Wirtschaftsstandort Japan: Veränderte Rahmenbedingungen für den Markteintritt," in K. Bellmann and R. Haak (Hrsg.) *Management in Japan. Herausforderungen und Erfolgsfaktoren für deutsche Unternehmen in einer dynamischen Umwelt*, Wiesbaden, Gabler 2005, S. 49–70.

Schwalbe, H. (1989) *Japan*. München: Prestel.

Sebestyén, O. G. (1994) *Management-Geheimnis Kaizen. Der japanische Weg zur Innovation*, Vienna: Wirtschaftsverlag Ueberreuter.

Sethi, S. P., N. Namiki and C. L. Swanson (1986) *False Promise of the Japanese Miracle. Illusions and Realities of the Japanese Management System*. Boston: Caroline House Publications.

Shiba, T. and M. Shimotani (eds) (1997) *Beyond the Firm: Business Groups in International and Historical Perspective*. Oxford: Oxford University Press.

Shibata, H. (2000) "The Transformation of the Wage and Performance Appraisal System in a Japanese Firm", *International Journal of Human Resource Management*, 11(2), 294–313.

Shimizu, T. (1988) "Japanisches Management", in W. Busse von Colbe, K. Chmielewicz, E. Gaugler and G. Laßmann (eds) *Betriebswirtschaftslehre in Japan und Deutschland. Unternehmensführung, Rechnungswesen und Finanzierung*, Stuttgart: Poeschel, S. 173–91.

Shimotani, M. (1997) "The History and Structure of Business Groups in Japan", in T. Shiba and M. Shimotani (eds) *Beyond the Firm: Business Groups in International and Historical Perspective*. Oxford: Oxford University Press, pp. 5–28.

Shire, K (2003) Gesellschaft. in P. Kevenhörster, Pascha, W. Shire, A. Karen (eds) Japan. Wirtschaft, Gesellschaft, Politik, Opladen, Leske+Budrich, S. 179–258.

Shirubâ Sâbisu Shinkôkai (2000) Shirubâ sâbisu no aramashi [Grundzüge der Silberdienste]. Tôkyô: Eigenverlag.

Sim, A. B. (1977) "Decentralized Management of Subsidiaries and their Performance", *Management International Review*. 2, pp. 45–51.

Simon, W. (ed.) (1969) Produktivitätsverbesserungen mit NC-Maschinen und Computern. Munich: Hanser.

Simon, H. (1986) Markterfolg in Japan. Strategien zur Überwindung von Eintrittsbarrieren. Wiesbaden: Gabler.

SMEA (Small and Medium Enterprises Agency) (1997) *White Paper on Small and Medium Enterprises*. Tokyo.

Smith, P. (1997) *Japan: A Reinterpretation*. New York: Pantheon.

Smitka, M. (1991) *Competitive Ties: Subcontracting in the Japanese Automotive Industry*. New York: Columbia University Press.

Solis, M. (2003) "Adjustment Through Globalization: The Role of State FDI Finance", in U. Schaede and W. Grimes (eds) *Japan's Managed Globalization: Adapting to the Twenty-first Century*. Armonk: Sharpe, pp. 101–23.

Sômuchô Tôkeikyoku (2002) Nihon tôkei nenkan - Heisei 14-nen [Japan Statistical Yearbook 2003]. Tôkyô: Nihon Tôkei Kyôkai.

Spur, G. (1979) *Produktionstechnik im Wandel*. Munich and Vienna: Hanser.

Spur, G. (1991) *Vom Wandel der industriellen Welt durch Werkzeugmaschinen*. Munich and Vienna: Hanser.

Spur, G. (1998a) *Technologie und Management. Zum Selbstverständnis der Technikwissenschaften.* Munich and Vienna: Hanser.

Spur, G. (1998b) *Fabrikbetrieb.* Munich and Vienna: Hanser.

Spur, G. (ed.) (1994) *Fabrikbetrieb. Handbuch der Fertigungstechnik.* Munich and Vienna: Hanser.

Spur, G. and D. Specht (1990) *Die Numerische Steuerung – Fallstudie einer erfolgreichen Innovation aus dem Bereich des Maschinenbaus.* Berlin: Akademie der Wissenschaften zu Berlin.

Spur, G. and F.-L. Krause (1997) *Das virtuelle Produkt.* Munich and Vienna: Hanser.

Staehle, W. (1999) *Management.* Munich: Vahlen.

Statistics Bureau (2003) *Japan Statistical Yearbook 2004.* Tokyo.

Steinmann, H. and G. Schreyögg (1997) *Management.* Wiesbaden: Gabler.

Stern, R. M. (ed.) (2003) *Japan's Economic Recovery: Commercial Policy, Monetary Policy, and Corporate Governance.* Cheltenham: Edward Elgar.

Stopford, J. and L. Wells Jr (1972) *Managing the Multinational Enterprise: Organization of the Firm and Ownership of the Subsidiaries.* New York: Basic Books.

Sugimoto, Y. (2003) *An Introduction to Japanese Society.* 2nd edition, Cambridge: Cambridge University Press.

Sullivan, J. J. (1992) "Japanese Management Philosophies: From the Vacuous to the Brilliant", *California Management Review* 34(2), pp. 66–87.

Suzuki, Y. (1991) *Japanese Management Structures, 1920–1980,* Houndsmills, London: Macmillan.

Suzuki, Y. (1994) *Nihon Teki Seisan Shisutemu to Kigyo,* Sapporo: Hokkaido Daigaku Tosho Shuppan Kai.

Suzuki, Y. (2004) "Structure of the Japanese Production System: Elusiveness and Reality", *Asian Business & Management,* 3, pp. 201–19.

Sydow, J. (1992) *Strategische Netzwerke – Evolution und Organisation,* Wiesbaden: Gabler.

Tachiki, D. (1991) "Japanese Management Going Transnational", *Journal for Quality and Participation.* 14, pp. 96–107.

Takahashi, Y. (1985) "Merkmale des Japanischen Managements unter besonderer Berücksichtigung des Personalmanagements", in S.-J. Park and H.-P. Merz (eds) *Transfer des Japanischen Management Systems.* Berlin: Express Edition, pp. 39–60.

Takamiya, S. and K. Thurley (1985) *Japan's Emerging Multinationals: An International Comparison of Policies and Practices,* Tokyo: University of Tokyo Press.

Takayama, K. (1997) "Machine Tool Industry", in Ifo Institute for Economic Research and Sakura Institute of Research (ed.) *A Comparative Analysis of Japanese and German Economic Success,* Tôkyô: Sakura Institute of Research, pp. 427–40.

Takeuchi, J. (1999) "Historical Features of Japanese Small and Medium Enterprises: A Comparative Economic Approach", in K. Odaka and M. Sawai (eds) *Small Firms, Large Concerns: The Development of Small Business in Comparative Perspective,* Oxford: Oxford University Press, pp. 197–216.

Taylor, F. W. (1903) *Shop Management.* New York: Harper & Brothers.

Taylor, F. W. (1911) *The Principles of Scientific Management*. Westport, Conn.: Greenwood Press.

Taylor, B. (2001) "The Management of Labour in Japanese Manufacturing Plants in China", *International Journal of Human Resource Management* 12(4), pp. 601–20.

Taylor, V. (2003) "Re-regulating Japanese Transactions: The Competition Law Dimension", in J. Amyx and P. Drysdale (eds) *Japanese Governance: Beyond Japan Inc.*, London: RoutledgeCurzon, pp. 134–55.

Teicher, K. (2005) "Human Resource Management deutscher Unternehmen in Japan", in K. Bellmann and R. Haak (Hrsg.) *Management in Japan*. Herausforderungen und Erfolgsfaktoren für deutsche Unternehmen in einer dynamischen Umwelt. Wiesbaden: Gabler, S. 163–76.

The Economist (11.02.2006) The fertility bust, S. 32.

Thomas, G. and Thomas, K. (1999) *Reisegast in Japan*. München: Iwanowski Reisebuchverlag.

Thurow, L. (1993) *Head to Head. The Coming Economic Battle among Japan. Europe, and America*. New York: Warner Books.

Toyoda, E. (1987) *Fifty Years in Motion*. Tokyo: Kodansha International.

Traphagan, J. W. and J. Knight (eds) (2003) *Demographic Change and the Family in Japan's Aging Society*. Albany: State University of New York Press.

Trevor, M. (1983) *Japan's Reluctant Multinationals: Japanese Management at Home and Abroad*. New York: St. Martin's Press.

Tsurumi, Y. (1976) *The Japanese are Coming: A Multinational Interaction of Firms and Politics*. Cambridge, MA: Ballinger Publishing Company.

Tsuruta, T. (1988) "The Rapid Growth Era", in R. Komiya, M. Okuno, K. Suzumura (eds) *Industrial Policy in Japan*, Orlando, FL: Academic Press, pp. 49–87.

Types and Numbers of Ports.

Upham, F. K. (1987) *Law and Social Change in Postwar Japan*. Cambridge: Harvard University Press.

Vaubel, D. (1986) Methoden des Markteintritts in Japan, in H. Simon (Hrsg.) *Markterfolg in Japan*. Strategien zur Überwindung von Eintrittsbarrieren: Wiesbaden: Gabler, S. 75–93.

Vaubel, D. and S. Höffinger (2003) Was in Japan tatsächlich (noch) anders ist. Studie, Tokyo: Roland Berger Strategy Consultants.

Vestal, J. E. (1993) *Planing for Change. Industrial Policy and Japanese Economic Development 1945–1990*. Oxford: Oxford University Press.

Visser "T Hooft, W. M. (2002) *Japanese Contract and Anti-Trust Law: A Sociological and Comparative Study*. London: RoutledgeCurzon.

Vogel, E. F. (1979) *Japan as Number One. Lessons for America*. Cambridge, Mass.: Harvard University Press.

Vogel, E. F. (1987) "Japan: Adaptive Communitarianism", in G. C. Lodge and E. F. Vogel (eds) *Ideology and National Competitiveness. An Analysis of Nine Countries*, Boston: Harvard Business School Press, pp. 141–72.

Waldenberger, F. (1994) "Grundzüge der Wirtschaftspolitik", in Deutsches Institut für Japanstudien (ed.) *Die Japanische Wirtschaft heute*. Munich: Iudicium, pp. 23–44.

Waldenberger, F. (1996) "Die Montageindustrien als Träger des japanischen Wirtschaftswunders. Die Rolle der Industriepolitik", in W. Schaumann (ed.) *Gewollt oder geworden? Planung, Zufall, natürliche Entwicklung in Japan.* Munich: Iudicium, pp. 259–71.

Waldenberger, F. (1998) "Wirtschaftspolitik", in Deutsches Institut für Japanstudien (ed.) *Die Wirtschaft Japans. Strukturen zwischen Kontinuität und Wandel.* Berlin: Springer, pp. 19–54.

Watanabe, T. (2003) "Recent Trends in Japanese Human Resource Management: The Introduction of a System of Individual and Independent Career Choice", *Asian Business & Management*, 2(1), pp. 111–41.

WEF (World Economic Forum) (2003) *The Global Competitiveness Report 2002–2003.* Oxford.

Westney, D. E. (2001) "Japanese Enterprise Faces the Twenty-First Century", in P. DiMaggio (ed.) *The Twenty-First Century Firm: Changing Economic Organization in International Perspective.* Princeton: Princeton University Press, pp. 104–43.

Whitehill, A. (1991) *Japanese Management: Tradition and Transition.* London: Routledge.

Winkels, U. and Y. Schülermann-Sugiyama (2000) *Verhandeln mit Japanern.* Wiesbaden: Gabler.

Womack, J. P. and D. T. Jones (1996) *Lean Thinking: Banish Waste and Create Wealth in Your Corporation.* New York: Simon & Schuster.

Womack, J. P., D. T. Jones and D. Ross (1990) *The Machine that Changed the World.* New York: Rawson.

Woronoff, J. (1992) *The Japanese Management Mystique. The Reality Behind the Myth.* Chicago, Cambridge: Irwin Professional.

Yamamura, K. and W. Streeck (eds) (2003) *The End of Diversity? Prospects for German and Japanese Capitalism.* Ithaca: Cornell University Press.

Yamashiro, A. (1997) *Japanische Managementlehre, Keieigaku.* Munich: Oldenbourg.

Yanagida, Y., D. H. Foote, E. S. Johnson, Jr., J. M. Ramseyer and H. T. Scogin, Jr. (1994) *Law and Investment in Japan: Cases and Materials.* Cambridge, Mass.: Harvard University Press.

Yanashita, K. (2001), *Wakariyasui Jinji ga Kaisha o Kaeru* [Simple HRM Can Change a Company]. Tôkyô: Nihon Keizai Shimbunsha.

Yashiro, N. (2003) "Demographic Changes and Their Implications for Japanese Household Savings", in R. M. Stern (ed.) *Japan's Economic Recovery: Commercial Policy, Monetary Policy, and Corporate Governance.* Cheltenham: Edward Elgar, pp. 375–95.

Yoshida, M. (1987) *Japanese Direct Manufacturing Investment in the United States,* New York: Praeger.

Yoshihara, H. (1995) "Management Localization and Performance of Overseas Japanese Companies", *Association of Japanese Business Studies Best Papers Proceedings*, Eighth Annual Meeting, Ann Arbor, Michigan, pp. 145–56.

Yoshikazu, Goto (2002) "Aging Populations, New Business Opportunities and New Business Models Developed in Japan," *Journal of Japanese Trade & Industry*, 3, S. 24–7.

Yoshimura, N. and P. Anderson (1997) *Inside the Kaisha: Demystifying Japanese Business Behavior*. Boston: Harvard Business School Press.

Yoshino, M. (1976) *Japan's Multinational Enterprises*. Cambridge, MA: Harvard University Press.

Yui, T. (1999) "Japanese Management Practices in Historical Perspective", in D. Dirks, J. F. Huchet and T. Ribault (eds) *Japanese Management in the Low Growth Era. Between External Shocks and Internal Evolution*. Berlin, Heidelberg and New York: Springer, pp. 13–18.

Zentes, J. B. Swoboda and D. Morschett (Hrsg.). Kooperationen, Allianzen und Netzwerke: Grundlagen – Ansätze – Perspektiven, Wiesbaden: Gabler 2003.

Index